James R. Parsons

French Schools Through American Eyes

A report to the New York state Department of public instruction

James R. Parsons

French Schools Through American Eyes

A report to the New York state Department of public instruction

ISBN/EAN: 9783337212186

Printed in Europe, USA, Canada, Australia, Japan

Cover: Foto ©Paul-Georg Meister /pixelio.de

More available books at **www.hansebooks.com**

FRENCH SCHOOLS
THROUGH AMERICAN EYES

A Report to the New York State Department
of Public Instruction

—BY—

JAMES RUSSELL PARSONS, JR.,

INSPECTOR OF TEACHERS' CLASSES, AND FORMERLY U. S.
CONSUL AT AIX-LA-CHAPELLE (AACHEN)

SYRACUSE, N. Y.:
C. W. BARDEEN, PUBLISHER
1892

Copyright, 1892, by C. W. BARDEEN

PREFACE

This account of the French elementary school system was prepared at the request of the Honorable Andrew S. Draper, Superintendent of Public Instruction for the State of New York, and appears in the thirty-eighth annual report, transmitted to the Legislature Jan. 20, 1892.

The following extract from Superintendent Draper's report explains itself :—

Comparisons of our own school system with those of other States or of foreign countries are interesting and instructive, and afford us some means of determining the wisdom of our efforts to provide the best possible educational advantages for the children of the State. Something can be gained from the study of the official foreign reports, much more by actual visitation of foreign schools and contact with their school officers and teachers.

In 1889, a commission appointed to make inquiry and report to the Legislature of Pennsylvania published an exhaustive report on the condition of industrial education in this country and in Europe.

In 1884, the New York Legislature considered, but did not pass a bill providing for the creation of a commission to examine the school system in this State and of such other States and countries as might be deemed expedient and necessary. The commission was to report such changes in the school system of the State as were deemed wise, and $8,000 were to be appropriated for salaries and expenses of the three commissioners.

Commissions, if composed of persons thoroughly fitted for the work, must of necessity involve considerable expense. In the absence of legislation in this direction, the Department has been fortunate in obtaining, virtually without cost to the State, comprehensive and detailed descriptions of the plan of organization and of the operations of school systems in foreign countries.

The report submitted in 1891 contained a well considered account of Prussian elementary schools, which has attracted much attention in educational circles throughout the country. It was prepared, at my request, by J. Russell Parsons, Jr., A. M., school commissioner in Rensselaer county from 1885 to 1888, and student of European school systems and United States Consul at Aix-la-Chapelle from 1888 to 1891.

The present report is accompanied by a scholarly paper on primary instruction in France (Appendix, Exhibit No. 4), which was also prepared, at my request, by Mr. Parsons, now one of the inspectors of teachers' training classes.

Mr. Parsons visited France during the last summer for the purpose of studying the French school system. His report is surprising in the clearness and perspicuity of its statements as well as in its completeness and comprehensiveness, and affords us valuable aid in determining our own procedure.

These two papers give a clear idea of the educational systems of the two leading countries of Europe which pay the closest attention to elementary schools. In the consideration of subjects connected with the schools of New York and in the statistics presented in this report, frequent occasion is found for reference to the organization and operations of the Prussian and French elementary schools, as they prove convenient and instructive standards of comparison.

I may add of this what I said of the German report of last year, that it is altogether the clearest statement that has ever appeared in English of just what these schools are doing.

SYRACUSE, *Feb. 3, 1892.*   C. W. BARDEEN.

PRIMARY INSTRUCTION IN FRANCE.

CONTENTS.

	PAGE.
Preface	7–9
Introduction	9–11

FIRST CHAPTER.
Political organization 11–13

SECOND CHAPTER.
Establishments for primary instruction 13–15

THIRD CHAPTER.
General development 15–19

FOURTH CHAPTER.
Population of France (*not including Algeria*) 19–22
School population 20–22
Density of population 22

FIFTH CHAPTER.
Number and division of institutions for primary instruction 23–26
Écoles maternelles 23
Lower and upper primary schools 23
Division of public primary schools 23
Division of private primary schools 23
Condition of schools 24
Classes 24–26
Écoles maternelles 24
Lower and upper primary schools 24–26
Teachers 26
Écoles maternelles 26
Lower and upper primary schools 26
Ratio between teachers and pupils 26

SIXTH CHAPTER.
Statistics relating to the preparation of teachers 27–28
Males 27
Females 27
Facilities for professional training 27, 28
Teachers' examinations 28

SEVENTH CHAPTER.

Statistics relating to inspection 28, 29
Cost of primary inspection 29

EIGHTH CHAPTER.

Statistics relating to auxiliary institutions 30–33
Classes of adults 30
School libraries 30, 31
Pedagogic libraries 31
School savings banks 31, 32
Caisses des écoles 32
Museé pédagogique 32, 33
Miscellaneous 33

NINTH CHAPTER.

Statistics showing the condition of primary instruction in Algeria 33

TENTH CHAPTER.

Private schools 34–35

ELEVENTH CHAPTER.

Establishment and maintenance of public schools 35–37

TWELFTH CHAPTER.

Inspection 38–41
Regulation of inspection 41

THIRTEENTH CHAPTER.

Teachers' conferences 41, 42

FOURTEENTH CHAPTER.

The teaching force 42–52
General certificates 42–46
Special certificates 46–50
Classes of teachers — Penalties and recompenses 50–52

FIFTEENTH CHAPTER.

Compulsory education 52–58
Commissions scolaires 53, 54
Certificate of primary studies 54, 55
Other provisions of the compulsory education law 56–58

SIXTEENTH CHAPTER.

Expenses of public primary instruction and salaries ... 58–63
Salaries 60–63
Observations 63

SEVENTEENTH CHAPTER.

Military service	63, 64
Observations	64

EIGHTEENTH CHAPTER.

Pensions	64, 65

NINETEENTH CHAPTER.

Écoles maternelles and classes enfantines	65–77
General organization	65–67
Pedagogic organization	67–72
Construction and furniture of écoles maternelles	72–77
General conditions	72, 73
Exercise halls	73, 74
Court, kitchen and play-ground	74
Privies	74, 75
Lodgings	75
Furniture	75, 76
Covered court	76
Supplies	77
Observation	77

TWENTIETH CHAPTER.

Lower primary schools	77–111
General and pedagogic organization	77–87
Division of the course of study in lower primary schools	87–92
Physical education	87, 88
Intellectual education	88, 89
Moral education	90–92
Construction and furniture of lower primary schools	92–97
General conditions	92, 93
Lodgings of the concierge	93
Cloak-rooms — Halls — Stairways	93, 94
Class	94, 95
Salle for drawing — Workshop for manual training	95
Covered court (préau) — Dependencies of the préau — Gymnasium	95
Playground — Garden	95
Privies and urinals — Vaults	96
Lodgings of teacher — Lodgings of assistant teachers	96
Furniture and teaching supplies	96, 97
Official programs of instruction in lower primary schools	98–109
Physical education	98, 99

	PAGE.
Intellectual education	100-106
Moral education	106-109
Time-tables in lower primary schools	110, 111

TWENTY-FIRST CHAPTER.

Upper primary schools and cours complémentaires	111-121
Official programs of instruction in upper primary schools and cours complémentaires.	113-121
Physical education and preparation for professional apprenticeship	113, 114
Intellectual education	114-120
Moral education	120, 121

TWENTY-SECOND CHAPTER.

Schools for industrial and commercial training	121, 123
Industrial schools and classes	121
Commercial schools and classes	122
Observation	122, 123

TWENTY-THIRD CHAPTER.

Primary normal schools	123-135
Students	124, 125
Course of study in primary normal schools	126-135
Normal schools for males	127-134
Normal schools for females	134, 135
Conclusion	135, 136

PRIMARY INSTRUCTION IN FRANCE.

"L'objet de l'enseignement primaire n'est pas d'embrasser sur les diverses matières auxquelles il touche tout ce qu'il est possible de savoir, mais de bien apprendre dans chacune d'elles ce qu'il n'est pas permis d'ignorer." — GRÉARD.

PREFACE.

The belief that everything American is perfect constitutes a form of false patriotism which seems to be growing in this country, particularly in the field of journalism. There is a large and increasing class of men who can not bear an adverse opinion touching anything American "without falling into those hysterics of holy horror, which are the usual refuge of ignorance and stupidity." If we are to realize, however, the promise of becoming the greatest nation in the world, we must cultivate the power of discrimination. We must learn to reject that which is bad; to adopt and perfect that which is good wherever it may be found. "The true greatness of a people," said M. Victor Cousin in 1833, "does not consist in borrowing nothing from others, but in borrowing from all whatever is good, and in perfecting whatever it appropriates."

There is no branch of the public service in which this power of discrimination is more needed than in primary instruction. France has succeeded in assimilating all that is good in the systems of elementary education of other countries without destroying the unity of her national character. What France has done, New York can and should do.

The problem of the French and Prussian teacher is to accomplish a fixed amount of work in a set time with a given number of children between fixed ages, who must attend school regularly. What is the problem confronting the New York teacher? To accomplish an indefinite amount of work in an indefinite time with an indefinite number of pupils between five and twenty-one years of age, who attend school when they feel disposed to do so. Compared with this, the secrets of perpetual motion and of the squaring of the circle are as nothing.

Whatever may be the opinions as regards secondary and higher education, the extent to which they should be gratuitous, the fields into which they should be carried by the State, almost all civilized people are unanimous in recognizing the universal necessity of an elementary education in those schools which represent the body of the nation. In order to make good and intelligent citizens, a minimum of school work is essential, and the most enlightened have now settled on the period of seven or eight years for its accomplishment.

As stated last year in my report on Prussian elementary schools, it would be most unjust to make an assertion that no good elementary school work is done in New York State. I have visited many schools in countries of the old world as well as in New York, and have never seen better elementary schools than the best schools here at home. More than this, I am aware that there are many schools to-day in obscure corners of my own county, or hidden among the hills of the school commissioner districts, which no thoughtful person can visit without being most favorably impressed by the faithful, conscientious and efficient work of the teachers. Working for very small salaries, struggling against the disadvantages of irregular attendance and a short school year, it is marvelous what these teachers accomplish.

But it is in vain that New York State goes on expending more and more each year for educational purposes. Without legislation insuring a full and regular attendance of the children from six to thirteen or fourteen years of age; without a minimum of qualifications for supervising officers as well as teachers; without an approximate equalization of local taxation for school purposes; without State supervision of instruction given in private schools and in families, we shall never attain anything approaching the uniform excellence of the work done in Prussian and French elementary schools.

The material for this report was taken from many sources. The principal references are to—

1. Nouveau Code de l'Instruction primaire. Pichard, Paris, 1890.
2. Annuaire de l'Instruction publique et des Beaux-arts. Delalain, Paris, 1891.
3. Les Traitements, le Classement, l'Avancement. Martel, Paris, 1890.
4. Éléments de Morale. Joly, Paris, 1887.
5. Statistique de l'Enseignement primaire. Ministère de l'Instruction publique et des Beaux-arts, Paris, 1889.
6. Quelques Mots sur l'Instruction publique en France. Bréal, Paris, 1885.
7. Nouveaux Programmes des Écoles primaires avec Divisions mensuelles et Emplois du Temps. Paris, 1889.
8. Manuel général de l'Instruction primaire. Journal hebdomadaire. Hachette, Paris, 1891.
9. Revue international de l'Enseignement. Colin, Paris, 1891.
10. Le Patriote. Bourde, Paris, 1888.
11. Travail manuel. Faivre, Paris, 1887.
12. La Leçon de Dessin dans les Écoles primaires et les Classes élémentaires de l'Enseignement secondaire. Leprat, Paris, 1889.

Throughout France there is at the present time a fermentation of thought in matters pertaining to public education. This is particularly true in cities and large centers of population. In speaking of the expense of public education in Paris, Albert Shaw says:

"Probably no other city in the world secures equally advantageous results from the outlay upon schools. Under the compulsory education act the attendance of children in elementary schools has actually been made almost universal. But Paris does not stop with elementary education in reading, writing and numbers. It maintains a marvelous system of industrial and trade schools for both sexes, in which almost everything that pertains to the production and traffic of Paris is taught and encouraged. American and English visitors at the exposition of 1889, will remember the remarkable display of the Paris industrial schools, especially in lines of decorative manufacture and art. It is in these schools that Parisian dressmakers, milliners, artificial-flower makers, furniture designers, house decorators, skilled workers in metals, and handicraftsmen in scores of lines of industry are educated to do the things that keep Paris prosperous and rich. It is public money wisely spent that maintains such an educational system. I need not refer to the higher schools of science, of classics and literature, of engineering and of fine art. All the flowers of civilization are encouraged by the Paris municipality. The yearly expenditure of a moderate but regular sum for the promotion of fine arts, by means of the purchase, under a competitive system, of designs for public statues, of pictures and mural designs for schools and various public buildings, and of other artistic works, not only educates the popular taste and adds to the adornment and beauty of the city, but helps to keep Paris the art center of the world, and thus to maintain what, from the economic point of view, is one of the chief and most profitable industries of Paris. The mercantile schools that train so many thousands of women as well as men in book-keeping and penmanship are also an admirable investment."

We turn now to the special consideration of what has been called the most complete national system ever devised, of compulsory, gratuitous and secular public education.

INTRODUCTION.

History teaches us that after great wars, and especially disastrous wars, public attention turns toward education. August 10, 1807, William III, King of Prussia, said: "The State must regain in intellectual force what it has lost in physical force." Men like Humboldt, Fichte and Stein were not wanting, and the result was the reorganization of national education, substantially completed in 1813.

The story of France from the close of the Franco-Prussian war is another striking illustration of this fact. For more than half a century the attention of the French people had been directed to the defects in their system of education. Strong men had devoted their lives to remedy these defects, and yet comparatively little was accomplished until France had been conquered by Prussia and her very existence was threatened.

The study of public education in France is particularly interesting to Americans. The laws, measures and methods, adopted by a sister republic to insure the requisite training for good and intelligent citizens, are not looked upon so suspiciously as those enforced under more despotic forms of government.

The documents setting forth the condition of public education in France are remarkable for precision, clearness and brevity. A study of the new code of primary instruction (*Nouveau Code de l'Instruction Primaire par A. E. Pichard*, 1890), will convince the New Yorker that our code should be thoroughly revised. It is a brave man, indeed, who has courage enough to venture an opinion on school matters in New York. Statutes are often contradictory and we are in almost as bad a condition as the Prussians who have no code of public instruction at all, but are forced to depend on a few general laws and many local decrees. The French system of primary instruction, however, is so clearly set forth in the code that it is very easy to understand. As a consequence there is much less contention than in New York, and a great saving of time and money.

The object of this report is to state as clearly and as concisely as possible just what the French system of primary instruction is, and the results which are accomplished under this system.

As in my report on Prussian elementary schools, an attempt is made to state clearly and concisely the minimum of work required of each healthy French child, and the provisions by which the accomplishment of this work is secured. The reader follows the would-be teacher through the Kindergarten (*école maternelle*), the lower and upper primary schools, the normal school, and the final examinations.

In France as in Prussia primary instruction is secured by the State against all casualties. It is uniform and invariable, because the primary schools represent the body of the nation and are destined to nourish and to strengthen the national unity. Compulsory education laws necessitate a full and regular attendance of the children of school age. Official courses of study fix the work to be accomplished in each of the different grades of schools. Teaching is elevated to the dignity of a profession and the tenure of office is secure. The State is most generous in supporting schools in poor and thinly populated districts. Trained teachers are found in rural as well as in city districts and the school year is at least forty weeks in length. The State supervises the instruction of children of school age in private schools and families, insisting on definite qualifications for private instructors. A minimum of qualifications is established for all teachers and inspectors of schools. Special teachers must hold the certificate of capacity for their particular lines of work.

These in brief are the principal advantages of the French elementary school system. New York elementary schools will never compare favorably with those of France without similar provisions. Since 1871 the standard of work done in French elementary schools has advanced with a rapidity which is without a parallel in the history of education, and which would seem entirely incredible to those not familiar with the tremendous sacrifices the Republic has made since the war.

Careful readers of the courses of study contained in this report will criticise the methods pursued in certain subjects. As a whole, however, these courses of study offer many interesting and valuable suggestions, particularly in the line of practical work.

FIRST CHAPTER.
POLITICAL ORGANIZATION.

France is divided into ninety departments (including the three departments of Algeria). Each department is subdivided into *arrondissements*, these into *cantons*, and the *cantons* into *communes*.

At the head of public instruction stands the minister (*Ministre de l'Instruction publique et des Beaux-arts*). Next to him come the director of higher education, the director of secondary education, and the director of primary education. These officers are assisted by inspectors general, assigned by the minister to certain departments at the beginning of each year.

The general administration is materially aided by the higher council (*conseil supérieur*), a dignified body composed of the leading educators of France, which assembles twice a year under the minister as chairman. The minister has power to call extra sessions.

The members of the higher council are appointed for four years. Nine councilors, appointed by the president of the republic, and six designated by the minister from the elected members, constitute the permanent section of the council. This permanent section meets every week and advises concerning courses of study and regulations; the creation, transformation and suppression of schools and colleges; text-books and books for libraries and prizes which are to be rejected by public schools; finally, all questions of instruction, administration and discipline suggested by the minister.

The whole council comprises sixty members, more than thirty of whom are professors and representatives of various educational institutions, chosen by their colleagues. Six, connected with primary education, are elected by the officers of primary education.

Four, connected with private instruction, are appointed by the president on the recommendation of the minister. Five are members of the institute and are elected by the institute.*

The higher council advises concerning courses of study, methods of instruction and modes of examination, and regulations, already deliberated on in the permanent section; regulations relative to the supervision of public schools; text-books, books for general reading and prizes, which should be rejected by public schools as contrary to morals, the constitution and the laws; rules relating to foreigners demanding an authorization to teach or open or direct a school.

The higher council is the court of last resort in the case of judgments rendered by the academic councils on matters of contention and discipline. It is also the final court of appeal from decisions of department councils in the case of expulsion of teachers.

A glance at the *Annuaire de l'Instruction publique* for 1891 will establish the fact that the most distinguished of French educators are members of this higher council.

Turning now from the general administration to the departments, we find these grouped into seventeen districts (including Algeria), called *académies*. The *Académie de Paris* includes nine departments, that of Chambéry only two; the rest range from three to eight.

At the head of the *académie* stands the rector, who is aided by the academic council (*conseil académique*), composed of secondary school officials of the several departments, members elected by their colleagues, and six members appointed by the minister.

An academy inspector (*inspecteur d'académie*) is placed over each department. He is assisted by the inspectors of primary instruction, and by the department council (*conseil départemental*).

The department council is a council of primary instruction, under the prefect† as president and the academy inspector as vice-president. The members are fourteen‡ in number, including four councilors general elected by their colleagues; the director of the normal school for males, the directress of the normal school for females; two male and two female teachers elected by the public school teachers (*titulaires*) of the department from among the directors or directresses of schools or from retired male or female teachers; two inspectors of primary instruction appointed by the minister. In cases of contention and discipline touching private

---

* The *Institut de France* comprises the *Académie française; des Inscriptions et Belles-lettres; des Sciences; des Beaux-arts; des Sciences morales et politiques.* Each of the five divisions meets once a week. Of the five members of the *Conseil supérieur*, one is chosen from each of the five divisions at a general session.

† The prefect (*préfet*) is the chief executive officer of a department.

‡ Increased in the *Département de la Seine*.

schools, two members, one from the clergy, the other from the laity, are elected by their respective colleagues.

Members of the department council are elected for three years. They receive no salary except traveling expenses in certain cases. The council meets four times a year, but special sessions may be called by the prefect. The meetings are not public. A majority of the members constitute a quorum.

The department council supervises the carrying out of courses of study, methods of instruction and rules, prescribed by the higher council, including the arrangements for medical supervision: deliberates touching the reports and propositions of the academy inspector; advises concerning reforms deemed necessary in the plan of instruction; discusses annually the general report of the academy inspector on the condition and needs of the public schools and on the condition of private schools; authorizes several communes to unite for the establishment and maintenance of a school; establishes schools with the approval of the minister, and determines their number, nature and location; may delegate to one-third of its members the right to inspect public and private schools; may authorize a male teacher to direct a mixed school; advises as to the number of pupils normal schools may receive; draws up rules for the public *écoles maternelles;* makes the list of teachers eligible to full instalment (*titulaires*); draws up rules for upper primary schools; advises touching the removal of directors and teachers of upper primary schools and schools of manual training; judges opposition made to the opening of private schools; authorizes private schools to receive children of both sexes; pronounces sentence in disciplinary cases; advises touching the authorization of foreigners to teach; fixes the number of assistant teachers with the approbation of the minister; determines the number of pupils and teachers in private boarding schools.

SECOND CHAPTER.
ESTABLISHMENTS FOR PRIMARY INSTRUCTION.

Primary instruction is given:

1. In Kindergärten (*écoles maternelles*) and infant classes (*classes enfantines*).

The *écoles maternelles* are Kindergärten for children of both sexes from 2 to 6 years of age.*

---

* These *motherly schools* are similar to, though not exactly the same as the German Kindergärten. As the name indicates, they are planned to follow the form of training adopted by an intelligent and devoted mother.

The *classes enfantines*, annexed to a lower primary school or to a Kindergarten, are for children of both sexes from 4 to 7 years of age. These infant classes form the mean between the Kindergarten and the primary school.

2. In the lower primary schools (*écoles primaires élémentaires*).

The lower primary schools are open to children from 6 to 13 years of age. No pupil may be admitted before the age of 6 years, if there exist in the community at a convenient distance a public *école maternelle;* before the age of 7 years, if there exist a public *classe enfantine.*

3. In the upper primary schools (*écoles primaires supérieures*), and in the complementary courses (*cours complémentaires*) annexed to the elementary schools.

The upper primary schools and the complementary courses receive only those children who have gained the certificate of primary studies (*certificat d'études primaires,* page 54).

4. In the schools of manual training (*écoles manuelles d'apprentissage*), as defined by the law of December 11, 1880.

The schools of manual training are designed to develop technical aptitude and to complete from a special point of view the instruction of the elementary schools. They receive children holding the certificate of primary studies or aged at least 13 years. By decree of July 28, 1888, no child under 12 may be admitted. The course of study covers at least three years.

5. In classes of adults and apprentices. These classes are not permitted to receive pupils under 13 years of age. They are never mixed classes. The instruction given is practical with special reference to the trades.

All establishments for primary instruction may be either public, that is founded and maintained by the State, the department and the communes, or private, that is founded and maintained by private individuals or associations.

Teachers and directors of public or private schools must be of French birth, and must meet the conditions of age and capacity fixed by law. Naturalized citizens may be authorized by the minister with the advice of the department council to teach in private schools, but all teachers in public schools must be of French birth.

Instruction is given by males in boys' schools; by females in girls' schools, in Kindergärten, in infant classes, and in mixed schools. The wife, sister, or near relative of the director of a boys' school may teach as an assistant in said school. The department council may also permit a male to direct a mixed school on condition that he be assisted by an instructress in needlework.

No instructor under 18, and no instructress under 17, is permitted to teach in a primary school of any degree. The director of a school below the upper primary school must have attained the age of 21 years. The director of an upper primary school or of a school receiving boarders must be at least 25 years of age.

Article 17 of the law of October 30, 1886, confines all grades of public instruction to the laity. At the same time certain provisions were made for the gradual execution of the law. In boys' schools, five years were allowed for its complete accomplishment. In girls' schools no limit was set. A glance at the statistics will show what has been done toward the secularization of public instruction (page 16).

All French public elementary schools are entirely free. Books, paper, ink and school supplies generally are gratuitous. More than this, the children of indigent parents are furnished with warm food in winter, with shoes and with clothing. In Prussia, public primary instruction is now practically gratuitous,* but books and school supplies are furnished only to the children of the poor, who are also supplied with food and clothing that they may be enabled to attend the schools.

THIRD CHAPTER.
GENERAL DEVELOPMENT.

Every five years since 1877 the ministry of public instruction has published a detailed report of the condition of primary instruction in France. This period of five years is chosen to correspond with the enumeration of the inhabitants, which takes place once in five years.

The latest report, published in 1889 (*Statistique de l'Enseignement primaire — Paris, Imprimerie nationale*, 1889), is based on the

---

* " Der § 4 des Gesetzes gestattet von der an die Spitze gestellten grundsätzlichen Regel, dass die Erhebung eines Schulgeldes bei Volksschulen fortan nicht stattfindet, zwei Ausnahmen, indem er

1. die Zulässigkeit der Erhebung von Schulgeld für solche Kinder, welche innerhalb des Bezirks der von ihnen besuchten Schule nicht einheimisch sind.

2. im Uebrigen aber die Erhebung von Schulgeld nur einstweilen noch gestattet und zwar nur insoweit, als das gegenwärtig bestehende Schulgeld durch den Staatsbeitrag nicht gedeckt wird."— Ausführungsanweisung zum Gesetz vom 11. Juni 1888. See also Article II of Law of March 31, 1889 and subsequent decrees.

census of May 30, 1886, and shows great progress since 1882, the date of the previous report. The statistics contained in this report are the latest available. A report based on the census of 1891 will not appear in all probability before 1893.

In obedience to the law of August 9, 1879, seven normal schools for males and forty for females were established in France between 1882 and 1887.* At the close of 1887 there were 172 normal schools, of which 90 were for males and 82 for females.

The law of October 30, 1886, has caused a corresponding development in the upper primary schools. In 1887 these schools were 302 in number. Including the 431 *cours complémentaires*, upper primary instruction embraced 1,600 teachers and 38,000 pupils.

At the present time public opinion directs that instruction given in these upper primary schools be in the line of professional and industrial training. Proper advantages must be provided for the training of good workmen in agriculture, industry and commerce. The proof of this is found in the courses of study of these schools as well as in the establishment of the three great national technical schools of *Armentières*, *Vierzon* and *Voiron*.†

In 1882, there were in France (not including Algeria), 75,635 upper and lower primary schools; in 1887, there were 80,209, an increase of 3,711 public and of 863 private schools.

The number of confessional public primary schools was reduced through the new law from 11,265 to 9,097. The number of public primary schools under lay direction increased from 51,732 to 57,611. On the other hand the number of confessional private schools increased within this period from 8,160 to 9,565, while the private schools under lay direction decreased from 4,478 to 3,936.

In 1882, France had 5,052 motherly schools (*écoles maternelles*), which number was increased to 5,882 in 1887. These schools received 644,384 pupils in 1882, and 741,224 in 1887.

---

* A partial parallel is found in Prussia where twenty-four new normal schools were established between 1870 and 1876.

† By law of December 11, 1880, and by decree of March 17, 1888, the *écoles manuelles d'apprentissage* and the upper primary schools with technical courses were placed under the double authority of the minister of public instruction and the minister of commerce and industry. Up to November, 1888, only the three great technical schools referred to above and a few special technical schools such as those at *Boulogne-sur-Mer, Rouen, Havre, Reims, Valréas, Aire-sur-Adour* and *Bar-sur-Seine* had come under this double *régime*. The statistics here given include only the upper primary schools under the sole authority of the minister of public instruction.

The total number of primary teachers in 1882, including the *écoles maternelles*, was 132,536. In 1887 this total was increased to 145,668, of whom 103,008 were public and 42,660 private teachers.

The percentage of lay teachers in public primary schools was seventy-seven in 1882 and eighty-four in 1887.

The total number of primary pupils registered in 1882, not including the *écoles maternelles*, was 5,341,211. In 1887, this total was 5,526,365. The public schools under lay direction gained 294,786, while the confessional public schools lost 209,474. At the same time the private secular schools lost 43,537, and the private confessional schools gained 143,379.

But the ministry of public instruction is not satisfied with figures based on registration alone. In order to substantiate these figures, the actual attendance in the public primary schools throughout the Republic was taken three times within this period of five years, on a fixed day. The results on December 4, 1886, and June 4, 1887, showed an actual attendance of 91 per cent and 88 per cent respectively, of the total registration for December and June.

The law of June 1, 1878, touching the *Caisse des écoles*, has increased very materially the amount of capital invested in school property. The hundred five and one-half millions of dollars devoted between 1878 and 1888 to the construction, repair and equipment of school buildings, represents a sacrifice for which posterity will be grateful. Indeed, the large number of substantial public school buildings now furnishes a material proof of the definite establishment of national instruction, which had been so long in a precarious condition.

In 1882 the current expenditures for public primary instruction were $26,757,888. In 1887 the amount was increased to $34,580,103.* Of this total, $7,600,000 were expended voluntarily by the communes for the development and amelioration of school facilities.

The following table shows the current expenditures for public primary instruction from 1882 to 1888:

1882	$26,757,888
1883	27,004,811
1884	28,330,455
1885*	34,120,074
1886*	34,651,229
1887*	34,580,103

*Including contributions by communes for sundry expenditures of which no record was kept previous to 1885. This fact should be borne in mind in making comparisons.

Of the $34,580,103 expended in 1887, the communes paid 40.6 per cent, the departments 10.6 per cent, and the State 48.8 per cent.

Deducting the communal expenses (*dépenses diverses communales*) of which no records were kept prior to 1885, the percentages from the three sources for 1887 were 28.1, 12.4 and 59.5 respectively.

The relative increase in State aid since 1855 is shown in the following table:

	Communes.	Departments.	State.
1855	64.8	18.3	16.9
1867	68.1	16.6	15.3
1877	57.4	18.0	24.6
1882	20.5	13.3	66.2
1887	28.1	12.4	59.5

The facts which merit attention are the great changes in 1882, caused by the law making primary instruction gratuitous and by other new laws, and the increase in the effort made by the communes in 1887.

The current expenditure of $34,580,103 represented an outlay of eighty-nine cents *per caput* of population * in 1887, or eight dollars and three cents for each pupil enrolled in December in the public schools, including the *écoles maternelles* (4,306,100).

It is not to be overlooked, however, that the annual current expenditures do not include the $105,517,290 devoted by the *Caisse des écoles* between June 1, 1878, and December 31, 1887, to the construction, repair and equipment of primary schools, or the loan of $1,554,313 granted the departments by the State for the construction of normal schools.†

Of the $105,517,290 referred to in the preceding paragraph, 58.41 per cent was borne by the communes, 2.62 per cent by the depart-

---

* " *Population de la France*, 38,218,903 *et population européenne et israélite de l'Algérie* 464,767 = 38,683,670."—*Annuaire statistique de la France*, 1888.

† " *Du 1er juin 1878 au 31 décembre 1887, la Caisse des écoles a dépensé pour constructions, réparations, ameublements une somme (dépense effectuée ou engagée) de 527 millions et demi (sans compter les engagements pris par l'État envers les départements pour constructions d'écoles normales)* " *Statistique de l'enseignement primaire*.

ments and 38.97 per cent by the State; $91,415,694 were expended between June 1, 1878, and June 20, 1885, and $14,101,596 between June 28, 1885, and December 31, 1887.

Under the law, communes with no available funds to provide and maintain suitable schools must secure a loan from the State payable in from thirty to forty years. Inasmuch as several generations are to profit by these extraordinary expenses, they are not included in the annual current expenditures. This fact must not be forgotten in estimating the total cost of public primary instruction.

If we divide into ten equal portions the extraordinary expenses for construction, repair and equipment between 1878 and 1888, and add one portion or $10,707,160 to the current expenditure for 1887, the grand total for public primary education in 1887 is $45,287,263, which represents an outlay of one dollar and seventeen cents *per caput* of population.*

In every group of 1,000 primary schools, 832 are public and 168 are private. Assuming that the costs for each pupil in public and private schools are equal, the expenditures for private instruction were about $10,600,000 in 1887. On this basis, public and private primary instruction cost $55,887,263 in 1887, which represents an outlay of one dollar and forty-four cents *per caput* of population.

FOURTH CHAPTER.
POPULATION OF FRANCE.
(Not including Algeria.)

The census of December, 1881, gave France a domiciled population of 37,672,048, and a present population of 37,405,290. The corresponding figures for the census of May, 30, 1886, were 38,218,903 and 37,930,759 respectively.†

It will be seen that the rate of increase is less than that of most European countries.

---

* Eighty-six per cent of the total public current expenditure in 1887 was for primary instruction. Secondary and higher instruction are now making rapid progress in France. More than $13,000,000 have been expended in buildings, repairs and equipments since 1877, the State bearing about half the burden.

† The domiciled population (*population domiciliée*) is the legal population. The present population (*population présente*) is made up of those who were actually present in the various communes on the night of May 29-30, 1886.

Everywhere the population now tends to group itself into the cities and large villages. In France the slow rate of increase in the population complicates this situation. The rural districts are depopulated, and there is difficulty in securing laborers to till the soil.

SCHOOL POPULATION.

The school population is divided into four groups according to age, as shown in the following table:

	BOYS AND GIRLS.	1881-1882.	1886-1887.
From 2 to 6	Enumerated	2,794,398	2,818,007
	Registered at a primary school or *école maternelle*	1,101,928	1,124,618
From 6 to 11	Enumerated	3,334,337	3,395,645
	Registered at a primary school	3,439,369	3,552,238
From 11 to 13	Enumerated	1,252,012	1,333,866
	Registered at a primary school	942,924	1,112,850
From 13 to 16	Enumerated	1,919,346	1,947,165
	Registered at a primary school	501,374	477,893
Summary	Total of children from 2 to 16	9,300,093	9,494,683
	Registered at an establishment of primary instruction	5,985,595	6,267,589

As groups two and three include the compulsory education period of seven years, from 6 to 13 years of age, they merit a more careful examination.

The population from 6 to 13 years of age is divided as follows:

	1881-1882.	1886-1887.
Boys	2,316,593	2,375,457
Girls	2,269,756	2,354,054
Total	4,586,349	4,729,511

As in almost all European countries, the number of boys in France slightly exceeds that of the girls. At birth there are about 105 boys for 100 girls, but during the first years of life the mortality of boys is greater than that of girls.

The following table from the last *Statistique de l'Enseignement primaire* will be of interest in showing the effectiveness of the compulsory education laws:

	1881-1882.	1886-1887.
Number of children from 6 to 13	4,586,349	4,729,511
Number of children from 6 to 13 registered as receiving instruction:		
In public and private *écoles maternelles*	85,170	113,795
In public primary schools	3,559,509	3,701,540
In private schools...	737,614	849,753
In secondary schools	43,397	77,975
At home (Law of March 28, 1882)......................		9,905
Total registration...	4,425,690	4,752,968

A comparison of the census for 1886, with the reported registration, shows an attendance of 23,457 in excess of the total number of children. This is attributed by the ministry to lack of precision in ascertaining and recording the ages of the children and to the reduplication of names. As a matter of fact, the number registered is always greater than the number actually in attendance during the year.

The number of children actually in attendance December 4, 1886, and June 4, 1887, was carefully ascertained by direction of the ministry in all the public primary schools. The former date is in the winter term, which is the period of full attendance; the latter, in the summer term, when, through agricultural duties, the attendance is somewhat smaller and more irregular. The results attained in this way differ very little from the general report. We are right, therefore, in concluding that the reported condition of the attendance on public schools merits all confidence. If we place the same value on the reported condition of the attendance on private schools, we may state that altogether, excluding the *écoles maternelles*, 91 per cent of the total number of children registered in December, 1886, were present December 4, 1886, and that 88 per cent of the total number registered in June, 1887, were present June 4, 1887.

The difference between the number registered and the number actually present in the upper primary schools is less than that in the lower primary schools, because the upper primary schools are situated in cities, where the general attendance is more regular than in the country, and because, as a rule, the pupils are more industrious than those of the lower primary schools. The upper primary schools, for example, registered 27,475 pupils in December, 1886, of which number 26,152 were present December 4, 1886; 25,276 pupils in June, 1887, of which number 23,749 were present June 4, 1887.

The difference, on the contrary, between registration and actual attendance in the Kindergärten (*écoles maternelles*) is greater. In December, 1886, 382,168 were registered, and 305,215 were present December 4. In June, 1887, 410,800 were registered and 338,280 were present June 4. It is to be added, however, that attendance on *écoles maternelles* is not compulsory, and that it is greatly reduced in bad weather.

DENSITY OF POPULATION.

In order to learn the needs of the various departments as regards school accommodations, we must study the statistics relative to the distribution of the inhabitants. In populous districts fewer schools are needed. The school must be at a convenient distance or pupils will either attend with difficulty or will not attend at all.

It is much cheaper relatively to provide school accommodations in populous districts than where the inhabitants are scattered over a large territory.

The area of France is 528,400 square kilometers. The average number of children from 6 to 13 years of age is nine per square kilometer. But in the different departments the school population varies greatly. The department of the Seine counts 581 children of this category, while other departments average but from six to two per square kilometer.

There were 36,121 communes in France in 1886–1887. The following table shows the population of these communes as compared with 1881–1882:

	1881–1882.	1886–1887.
From 12 to 400 inhabitants	13,271	13,562
From 401 to 500 inhabitants	3,599	3,619
From 501 to 1,000 inhabitants	10,633	10,362
From 1,001 to 5,000 inhabitants	8,059	8,016
From 5,001 to 10,000 inhabitants	312	328
From 10,001 to 20,000 inhabitants	132	134
Above 20,000 inhabitants	91	100
Total	36,097	36,121

FIFTH CHAPTER.
NUMBER AND DIVISION OF INSTITUTIONS FOR PRIMARY INSTRUCTION.

The several establishments of primary instruction are divided as follows:

1. ÉCOLES MATERNELLES.

	1881-1882.	1886-1887.
Public	3,161	3,447
Private	1,891	2,435
Total	5,052	5,882

2. LOWER AND UPPER PRIMARY SCHOOLS.

	1881-1882.	1886-1887.
Public	62,997	66,708
Private	12,638	13,501
Total	75,635	80,209

a. Division of public primary schools.

	1881-1882.	1886-1887.
Boys' schools	24,371	25,121
Girls' schools	21,504	23,224
Mixed schools	17,122	18,363
Total	62,997	66,708

b. Division of private primary schools.

	1881-1882.	1886-1887.
Boys' schools	2,195	2,521
Girls' schools	9,796	10,236
Mixed schools	647	744
Total	12,638	13,501

CONDITION OF SCHOOLS.

In 1887, 53,166 school buildings belonged to the communes.* The number of buildings rented or loaned diminished from 15,625 in 1882 to 13,344 in 1887. The condition of school buildings improved greatly during this period. There were 35,547 buildings in perfect repair in 1887 as against 29,355 in 1882. In 1887, 50,344 schools were provided with a garden (as against 42,586 in 1882); 5,592 with a gymnasium and 466 with a workshop for manual training.

CLASSES.

The classes in the several establishments of primary instruction are as follows:

1. Écoles Maternelles.

It is not possible to give the exact number of classes in these Kindergärten inasmuch as the division into two classes is not strictly followed in all. But as there are 3,447 directresses and 2,270 assistants in the 3,447 public *écoles maternelles*, and 2,435 directresses and 701 assistants in the 2,435 private *écoles maternelles*, it is certain that a large number of these institutions have in reality two classes.

2. Lower and Upper Primary Schools.

The following table shows the division of classes in the public and private primary schools:

	1881-1882.	1886-1887.
Schools with one class	53,295	54,516
Schools with two classes	13,073	14,959
Schools with three classes	4,553	5,024
Schools with four classes	2,063	2,410
Schools with five classes	1,120	1,275
Schools with six classes	716	883
Schools with seven classes	322	495
Schools with eight or more classes	493	647
Total	75,635	80,209

In 1887 there were 96,057 classes in the public primary schools under the charge of as many teachers.

---

*For purposes of comparison, the method of calculation used in 1882 is followed. Each *groupe scolaire* is counted as two schools. If counted as one school, there were 60,518 schools in 1887, of which number 47,174 belonged to the communes and 13,344 were loaned or rented.

These classes were divided as follows:

	1881-1882.	1886-1887.
Boys' classes	37,415	41,408
Girls' classes	32,009	36,024
Mixed classes	17,335	18,625
Total	86,759	96,057

In 84.7 per cent of the classes, the number of pupils did not exceed fifty; in 9.6 per cent, the number was between fifty-one and sixty; in 3.7 per cent, between sixty-one and seventy; in 1.3 per cent, between seventy-one and eighty; above eighty, in 0.7 per cent of the classes.

Like New York, France labors under a great disadvantage owing to the very unequal distribution of the inhabitants.

In 7,117 ungraded schools, the total number of pupils in 1887 averaged 14.7 for each school.

In 969 schools with two classes, there were less than 50 pupils.

In 109 schools with four classes, there were less than 120 pupils.

In 118 schools with five classes, there were less than 175 pupils.

In 54 schools with six classes, there were less than 210 pupils.

In 42 schools with seven or more classes, the average number of pupils per class was less than 35.

In 1887, there were 34,471 classes in the private primary schools. These classes were divided as follows:

Boys' classes	7,590
Girls' classes	25,751
Mixed classes	1,130
Total	34,471
Classes not exceeding fifty pupils	31,525
Classes with from fifty-one to sixty pupils	2,009
Classes with from sixty-one to seventy pupils	676
Classes with from seventy-one to eighty pupils	189
Classes with more than eighty pupils	72
Total	34,471

TEACHERS.

The teachers in the several institutions of primary instruction are classed as follows:

1. ÉCOLES MATERNELLES.

		Directresses.	Assistants.	Total.
Public schools	{ 1881-1882	3,161	1,836	4,997
	{ 1886-1887	3,447	2,270	5,717
Private schools	{ 1881-1882	1,891	683	2,574
	{ 1886-1887	2,435	701	3,136

By this table we see that there were 7,571 teachers in these Kindergärten in 1882, and 8,853 in 1887.

2. LOWER AND UPPER PRIMARY SCHOOLS.

	Male.	Female.	Total.
1881-1882	58,137	66,828	124,965
1886-1887	63,152	73,663	136,815

These teachers were divided between public and private schools in the following ratio:

	1881-1882.	1886-1887.
Public schools	88,220	97,291
Private schools	36,745	39,524
Total	124,965	136,815

RATIO BETWEEN TEACHERS AND PUPILS.

The reports of the number of public school teachers as compared with the number of children of school age show that in 1887 there was one male teacher for forty-three boys, and one female teacher for fifty-five girls. In 1882, these ratios were one to forty-six and one to sixty-one respectively. In Prussia, in 1886, the average number of pupils under one teacher was a fraction over seventy-four; in New York, forty-three (on average daily attendance 26).

SIXTH CHAPTER.
STATISTICS RELATING TO THE PREPARATION OF TEACHERS.
MALES.

In 1882 there were eighty-three normal schools for males. New schools were established in seven departments between 1882 and 1887.

In 1887 the ninety normal schools for males had 489 directors, stewards (*économes*) and assistants (*maîtres adjoints*), 606 professors (*externes*), and 5,443 students.

In 1882 the eighty-three normal schools for males had 4,767 students. In five years, therefore, the increase was 14.2 per cent.

Between 1882 and 1887, 8,054 students were graduated from these normal schools for males. Between 1877 and 1882, 6,105 students were graduated therefrom. The increase in the later period, therefore, was 31.9 per cent.

FEMALES.

In 1882 there were forty-one normal schools for females. Forty new schools were established between 1882 and 1887.

In 1887 the eighty-one normal schools for females counted 474 directresses, stewards and assistants (*maîtresses adjointes*), 415 professors (*externes*) and 3,544 students.

In 1882 the forty-one normal schools for females counted only 2,002 students. In five years, therefore, the rate of increase was 77 per cent.

Between 1882 and 1887, 4,285 students were graduated from the normal schools for females. Between 1877 and 1882, 1,310 students were graduated from these schools. The rate of increase in the later period, therefore, was 227 per cent.

FACILITIES FOR PROFESSIONAL TRAINING.

The object of the law of 1879 was nearly accomplished in 1887, when all departments of France and Algeria, except *Oran*, had a normal school for males, and all except *Alpes-Maritimes*, *Aveyron*, *Belfort*, *Creuse*, *Eure*,* *Indre*, *Tarn*, *Var* and *Constantine*, a normal school for females. Everywhere in a large measure and exclusively in some departments, recruits for the teaching force are now normal graduates, and normal school facilities are adequate to supply the demand for teachers.

---

* A normal school for females was finished in this department in October, 1888.

Under the new law the current expenses of the normal schools have increased from year to year. In 1882 the ordinary current expenses for normal schools amounted to $1,378,385. In 1887 the amount was increased to $1,880,095.

TEACHERS' EXAMINATIONS.

A study of the official reports of the examination of candidates for the *brevet élémentaire* and the *brevet supérieur* from 1882 to 1887 shows that from 25.6 per cent to 45.3 per cent of the males were successful, and that from 36.3 per cent to 56.7 per cent of the females were successful.

In 1882, 72.9 per cent of all public primary teachers held State certificates. In 1887 the percentage was increased to 90.8. In 1887, 79.3 per cent of all private primary teachers held State certificates; 85.9 per cent of all teachers in public *écoles maternelles* and 71.6 per cent of all teachers in private *écoles maternelles*.

SEVENTH CHAPTER.
STATISTICS RELATING TO INSPECTION.

Primary instruction in France is under the minister of public instruction.

The direction of primary instruction is divided between six departments. Six inspectors general are charged with the inspection of primary instruction in the seventeen *académies* (including Algeria). Three other general inspectors supervise, respectively, the management of the normal and technical schools; the manual training in the normal and upper primary schools; the instruction in gymnastics and military exercises in the various establishments of primary instruction.

The inspection of instruction in vocal and instrumental music, and the inspection of instruction in modern languages in the normal and upper primary schools are under special inspectors. The inspection of drawing in normal and upper primary schools is also confided to special inspectors of drawing.

There are four inspectresses general of the *écoles maternelles*.

In each department, the service of primary instruction is directed by an academy inspector. A council, called the department council, presided over by the prefect, gives opinions, takes evidence and renders decisions on questions within its province (page 12).

The primary inspectors, named by the minister, are subordinate to the rector and under the immediate orders of the academy inspector.

The primary inspectors correspond to school commissioners in New York. For details regarding the qualifications of these officers see page 39.

The number of primary inspectors for each year from 1882 to 1887 is given in the following table:

1882	455
1883	473
1884	475
1885	474
1886	474
1887	456

The area of France being 528,400 square kilometers, there was one primary inspector for each 1,159 square kilometers in 1887.

Inspection districts vary greatly in size and in number of schools. The mean is one inspector for 146 public primary schools, for 211 classes and 213 teachers of these schools, or for 189 schools of every kind (including *écoles maternelles*), for 286 classes and 319 teachers.

The largest districts are Marseilles with 860 and 579 classes; *Lille* 1st and *Lille* 2d, *Douai* and *Valenciennes*, with 829, 701, 506 and 644 respectively; *Rouen* 1st, with 634; *Courbevoie-Neuilly* and the 4th and 5th *arrondissements* of Paris, with 630 and 532 respectively.

The smallest districts are those of *Castellane, Sisteron* and *Loudun*, with 120, 127 and 118 respectively.

The mean of 146 public schools is too high. Recommendations have been made in the latest reports to reduce to 100 in order that the inspector may visit each school under his charge several times a year.

The attitude of the administration, however, is far from satisfactory in this respect. Eighteen inspectorships were discontinued in 1887, and twenty-seven have been suppressed for financial reasons since 1887.

Cost of Primary Inspection.

The cost of inspection is paid by the State. It amounted in 1882 to $429,271, and in 1887 to $428,935 (including Algeria).

There is general complaint at the false economy which has checked the growth of this most necessary feature of public school work.

EIGHTH CHAPTER.
STATISTICS RELATING TO AUXILIARY INSTITUTIONS.
CLASSES OF ADULTS.

The number of these classes for men and women was 28,835 in 1881-1882, and only 9,053 in 1886-1887. The decrease of 19,782 was due to the rigorous conditions imposed by the State as regards State aid, and also to the rapid development of primary instruction.

In 1881-1882, 596,322 persons frequented these classes; in 1886-1887, the number was reduced to 184,612.

By decree of April 4, 1882, these classes were divided into those in elementary work for the illiterate, and into those in special courses for the others in attendance.

In 1886-1887 there were 1,579 classes doing elementary work, and 7,474 special classes.

With the development of primary instruction, illiteracy decreases rapidly, and classes for the illiterate become unnecessary. These statistics are interesting, however, as an additional evidence of the tremendous sacrifices France is making for the education of her people.

SCHOOL LIBRARIES.

The following table shows the condition of the school libraries from 1882 to 1887:

	Number of libraries.	Number of volumes.	Number of loans.
1882	28,251	2,894,440	....
1883	28,845	3,160,823	3,082,486
1884	30,920	3,226,896	3,586,227
1885	32,302	3,852,541	4,157,786
1886	33,880	4,159,208	4,866,676
1887	34,992	4,410,242	5,421,634

In many localities, thanks to the choice of books, the taste of the inhabitants, or the zeal of the teacher, the library is in general demand. In other districts, as with us, the books seldom leave the shelves.

If these figures from the latest official statistics are reliable, and there seems to be no reason for doubt, the number of loans increased 76 per cent between 1887 and 1883, when the first reports of this kind were required.

We must admit that the above table shows steady progress. This is easily understood when we note the care taken by the authorities through wise counsels and prizes to encourage a taste for good reading.

PEDAGOGIC LIBRARIES.

These libraries which exist in most departments complement the teachers' conferences. Teachers desirous of completing their education or of extending their professional information find therein the necessary pedagogic works, including periodicals and official documents.

The following table shows the condition of these libraries from 1882 to 1887:

	Number of libraries.	Number of volumes.
1882	2,470	585,651
1883	2,500	663,878
1884	2,624	753,336
1885	2,577	803,419
1886	2,626	876,739
1887	2,654	889,183

In five years the number of libraries increased by 184, and the number of volumes by 303,532.

SCHOOL SAVINGS BANKS.

Caisses d'Épargne scolaires.

These banks are established voluntarily by teachers. The administration of public instruction encourages them with the idea that the promotion of a spirit of economy on the part of pupils may lead to the same habit and taste on the part of parents.

The following table shows the progress made between 1883 and 1888:

		Number of banks.	Number of books.	Amounts registered.
	1882	19,433	395,867	$1,812,917
	1883	21,481	442,021	2,049,665
	1884	23,222	458,624	2,257,009
Report for December 31	1885	23,980	491,160	2,386,853
	1886	23,375	484,162	2,467,631
	1887	22,385	478,173	2,536,663

The decrease in the number of school banks in 1886 and 1887 may be attributed to the fact that some teachers have substituted postal banks for school banks. Nevertheless, as will be seen, the amounts deposited have increased from year to year.

For further particulars relating to these school banks, see page 86. Facts like these serve to explain the ease with which the French people raise money in emergencies. They form and encourage the habit of saving if no more than penny by penny.*

CAISSES DES ÉCOLES.

The following table shows the condition of the *caisses des écoles* in January, 1883 and in January, 1888:

	December 31, 1882.	December 31, 1887.
Number of *caisses*	16,207	16,954
Values in *caisse* at the close of the preceding *exercice*, and total receipts of current *exercice*	$612,232	$1,021,671
Total expense of the *exercice*	305,332	703,684
Values in *caisse* at the close of the *exercice*	306,900	317,987

The law of March 28, 1882, made the establishment of a *caisse des écoles* obligatory for each commune. As the result, the 928 caisses in January, 1880, were increased to 16,954 in January, 1888.

MUSEE PEDAGOGIQUE.

This very useful institution is situated in Paris. It contains a very complete exhibit of models of schools, school furniture and school appliances from all parts of the world. Here may be found one of the best pedagogic libraries in existence, and most interesting specimens of work from the pupils of schools of different countries.

The museum is open daily, Sundays excepted, from 10 A. M. to 5 P. M. Admission is by card except on Thursday (1891).

It is now proposed to make a permanent exhibit of the *cahiers* of pupils from all French primary schools. Specimens of these blank-

---

* School savings banks are found in Belgium, England, Germany, Italy, Switzerland, Russia and other European countries. Thiry's "School Savings Banks in the United States" shows what has been done and what may be done in this country.

books of monthly tasks are to be deposited (if the plan is adopted) annually at the museum as an incentive to earnest effort, and as an indication of the progress made from year to year.

MISCELLANEOUS.

In addition to the auxiliary institutions mentioned above, there are thousands of museums accessible to the pupils and teachers. Many are directly connected with the schools.

The value of these institutions is shown in the high appreciation by the French people of works of art. This is largely due to the foundations laid in the primary schools.

Teachers' mutual aid societies,* the *Oeuvre de l'Orphelinat de l'Enseignement primaire*,† army and navy schools, asyla for the deaf and dumb, the blind and the insane, and reform schools are among the auxiliaries of primary instruction, too numerous to be set forth here in detail.

NINTH CHAPTER.

STATISTICS SHOWING THE CONDITION OF PRIMARY INSTRUCTION IN ALGERIA.‡

Inasmuch as public instruction in Algeria, by virtue of the decrees of 1883, is a part of that of France, we must review briefly the statistics from the three departments of Algeria, in order to present fully the condition of the schools under the direction and supervision of the minister of public instruction.

In October, 1887, the primary schools of Algeria numbered 1,129, as against 978 in 1882; 1,840 primary teachers, as against 1,492; 366 teachers of *écoles maternelles*, as against 296; 97,097 pupils, as against 78,016; 8,963 native pupils, as against 3,516.

Of the 33,917 French pupils of school age, 26,836, or 79 per cent, frequented the primary schools. There were also 1,400 pupils of school age in secondary schools.

The recruitment of the teaching force is assured in part by four normal schools; two for males and two for females. There are also two normal courses for native teachers annexed to the normal schools at Algiers and Constantine.

---

*Teachers' mutual aid societies are found in all departments of France except five. In 1887 these societies reported a capital of $807,354.

†This association has no orphanage, but provides for the care in private families of orphans whose parents were teachers or school officers.

‡France is now laboring strenuously to promote public education in her colonies and in the *pays de protectoral*.

TENTH CHAPTER.
PRIVATE SCHOOLS.

Directors of private schools are free to choose methods of instruction, courses of study and books, provided the books are not among those blacklisted by the higher council as contrary to morals, the constitution and the laws.

No private school may be given the title upper primary school unless the director hold the certificates required in the case of public upper primary schools.

No private school, without the authorization of the department council, may receive children of both sexes, if there exist in the locality a special public or private school for girls.

No private school may receive children under 6, if there exist in the commune a public *école maternelle* or *classe enfantine*, unless provided with a *classe enfantine*.

Every teacher desiring to open a private school must first declare his intention to the mayor of the commune, indicating the site for the school.

The mayor acknowledges formally the receipt of the declaration, which is posted at the entrance to the mayoralty for one month.

If the mayor find that the proposed site is not suitable for reasons touching morals or health, he opposes the opening of the school, informing the postulant within eight days after the declaration.

The same formal steps must be taken in case of a change in the location of a private school, or in case of the admission of boarders.

The postulant sends the same declaration to the prefect, the academy inspector and the government attorney. He submits also to the academy inspector his birth certificate, his diplomas, a statement of residence and work for ten preceding years, the plan of the school, and, if he belong to any association, a copy of the statutes of said association.

The academy inspector, either of his own accord, or on complaint of the government ttorney, may oppose the opening of the school on moral or sanitary grounds.

In the case of a dismissed public teacher, wishing to establish himself as private teacher in the district in which he once taught, the opposition may be made in the interest of public order.

In case no opposition is made, the school is opened at the expiration of the month without further formality.

In cases of opposition to the opening of private schools, decisions are given by the department council within a month. An appeal may be made from these decisions to the higher council. The school is not to be opened while the appeal is pending.

Failure to comply with these provisions subjects to fines of from $20 to $200. The school is closed. In case of the repetition of the offense, the delinquent is condemned to imprisonment for from six days to one month, and pays a fine of from $100 to $400. Extenuating circumstances meet consideration under article 463 of the penal code.

Every private teacher may be brought before the department council on complaint of the academy inspector, for any serious fault in the discharge of his duties, for misconduct or immorality. The department council may censure or may suspend, temporarily or permanently, according to the gravity of the offense. An appeal may be made to the higher council.

Every director of a private school refusing to submit to the supervision and inspection of the school authorities, under legal provisions, is fined from $10 to $100, and, for a second offense, from $100 to $200. Extenuating circumstances meet consideration under the section of the penal code referred to above. In case of two offenses in one year the establishment will be closed.

ELEVENTH CHAPTER.
ESTABLISHMENT AND MAINTENANCE OF PUBLIC SCHOOLS.

Every district (*commune*) should be provided with at least one public elementary school, but with the authorization of the department council and with the consent of the minister, several communes may unite in establishing and maintaining a school.

Several villages of a commune may be attached to the school of a neighboring commune by a decision of the interested communes. In case of a difference of opinion, this may be prescribed by a decree of the department council.

If the commune or union of communes have 500 inhabitants or more, it should have at least one special school for girls, unless authorized by the department council to substitute a mixed school.

The law of March 20, 1883 makes it obligatory on each commune to establish schools at the chief place in the commune and in the villages or centers of population at a distance of three kilometers from the said chief place or from each other, and embracing at least

20 children of school age. By law of October 30, 1886, the district of village schools so created may include portions of several communes. In this case as in the cases referred to above, the interested communes contribute toward the expense of building and maintaining the schools in the proportions determined by the municipal councils, and, in case of differences of opinion, by the prefect with the advice of the department council.*

The department council of public instruction, with the advice of the municipal councils and with the approval of the minister, determines the number, nature and location of the public primary schools of every degree, which each commune is to establish and maintain, and the number of teachers to be employed therein.

The expense of the establishment of public primary schools is to be borne by the communes. The lodging of the teaching force; the maintenance or rent of the buildings: the purchase and maintenance of the school furniture; the heating, lighting and janitor's fees must be paid by the communes. The same law also applies to public girls' schools now established in communes of more than 400 souls; to public motherly schools (*écoles maternelles*) which are or will be established in communes of more than 2,000 souls, having a close population of at least 1,200 souls;† to public *classes enfantines* embracing children of both sexes and taught by women.

By law of March 20, 1883, the expense of establishing a school is met either by levying on available funds of the commune or by a loan at the special *caisse* or by grants from the department and from the State.

The site for the school is designated by the municipal council, or, in default, by the prefect.

By law of April 7, 1887, the plans and estimates are prepared by the mayor and adopted by the municipal council. They are examined by the academy inspector who consults the department committee on public buildings. On the report of the academy inspector, the prefect determines whether the plans and estimates are to be accepted or whether the municipal council is to be requested to present others.

If the plans are to be accepted the municipal council is to vote the loans and provide the necessary resources.

---

* In 1887 there were 80 communes which had no schools and 67 which had only private schools. In 1882 the figures were 159 and 89 respectively.

† The law does not oblige communes to establish *écoles maternelles*, and they are not classed as public institutions in smaller communes.

When the municipal council has voted a loan for at least thirty years, destined to pay the whole or a part of the estimated expense, and has decided to demand aid from the state by virtue of the law of June 20, 1885, the prefect submits the claim to the general council at its next sesssion. If the council refuse or neglect to come to a decision, the prefect applies to the minister of public instruction.

If the minister approve all arrangements, including plans, specifications and estimates, he fixes the amount of the State grant according to decree of February 15, 1886, and determines the time for the completion of the work.

The work of construction is supervised by a member of the department committee on public buildings whose salary and expenses are included in the original estimate. The State makes no payments until the building is finished and approved, except on the certificate of this official that the work is being done according to contract.

By law of June 20, 1885, the proportion of the annuities paid by the State may not in any case exceed 80 per cent nor be less than 15 per cent, in accordance with the resources of the commune.

Communes whose *centime communal* represents a greater value than 6,000 francs, can not receive any aid from the State, either for the construction, reconstruction or enlargement of their primary schools.

Each year the budget of public instruction contains a special chapter on grants to departments, cities or communes, for the payment of a portion of the annuities due for the construction of public, high, secondary and primary schools.

The following table fixes the maximum amount toward which the State will contribute for the different classes of schools connected with primary instruction:

1. For a village school (ungraded) $2,400
2. For a school in the chief place of a commune (with one class either mixed or for girls or for boys) 3,000
3. For a *groupe scolaire*, with one class for each sex 5,600
4. For each class added to the *groupe scolaire*, or to a school in the chief place of a commune 2,400
5. For an *école maternelle* 3,600
6. For an upper primary school 16,000
7. For a normal school 80,000

TWELFTH CHAPTER.
INSPECTION.

Public and private primary schools are inspected:

1. *By the inspectors general of public instruction.*— These officers are appointed by the president of the republic on the recommendation of the minister. They are chosen from the rectors, academy inspectors, college professors, secondary school principals, inspectors of primary instruction and other officers whose qualifications are definitely fixed by law. At the commencement of each year the minister assigns to each of these officers the departments he is to visit. The condition of normal schools is determined by special inspection. Vocal and instrumental music, manual training and modern languages in normal schools and in upper primary schools are the objects of special missions, while the inspection of the drawing in these schools is confided to special inspectors, each one for the district to which he is attached. The inspectors general form a committee, under the director of primary instruction as chairman, to study questions submitted by the minister.

2. *By the rectors and academy inspectors.* — The rectors are appointed by the president of the republic on the recommendation of the minister.

They must have obtained the degree of doctor. The principal duties of rectors are to approve the list of books to be used in the public schools of each department; to appoint the commission for the examination of candidates seeking admission to the normal schools; to regulate promotion of students in normal schools; to name normal school physicians; to arrange the division of work in normal school faculties; to appoint examining committees for teachers' certificates and pupils' certificates. The academy inspectors are appointed by the minister. They must either have had ten years' experience in teaching or hold a diploma equivalent to our bachelor's degree. They are chosen from college professors, principals of secondary schools, inspectors of primary instruction and other school officers whose qualifications are defined by law. The principal duties of academy inspectors are to insure the execution of orders; to authorize public *écoles maternelles* to receive more than 150 children; to accord dispensations in age for teachers' certificates; to choose subjects for theses at examinations for teachers' certificates and school examinations; to report the results of teachers' examinations; to name the commission for examining teachers of needlework; to preside over the commissions for the certificate of *aptitude pédagogique*, and of admission to the normal school.

3. *By the inspectors and inspectresses of primary instruction.*— These officers are named by the minister. They must hold the certificate of fitness for the inspection of primary schools, and for the direction of normal schools. An annual examination is held for this purpose before a commission of five persons. Candidates must be at least 25 years of age. They must have had an experience of at least five years in teaching in public schools. During two of these years at least they must have directed a school. They must hold the certificate of fitness for a professorship in the normal schools, or the title of professor or bachelor of secondary instruction, or diplomas equivalent to our high school diplomas or bachelors' degrees. The examination is both oral and written, including a practical test. The oral examination embraces pedagogy, school law and school management. Candidates are required to explain a passage in one of the authors' designated for the year. They next draw by lot a question relative to some point included in the program of examinations, and, after three hours' reflection, this question is treated orally.

The written examination consists of two theses composed in two consecutive days, one on some pedagogic subject, the other on school administration.

The practical test lies in the inspection of a normal school, an upper primary school, a lower primary school or *école maternelle* followed by a verbal report (1887, 1888).

These officers correspond to our school commissioners. They are placed under the immediate authority of the academy inspector, and receive no instructions save from him, the rector, the inspectors general and the minister. They are not permitted to accept any other public position, except the inspection of children employed in manufactories. Their principal duties are to assure the execution of orders; to inspect new school buildings before they are opened; to inspect public and private schools; to control the classification and gradation of pupils; to approve the time-tables adopted by school directors; to authorize promotion from the *écoles maternelles* or the *classes enfantines* to the primary schools; to make a report to the academy inspector within fifteen days after each inspection; to supervise the formation and construction of public schools, the opening of private schools, of classes of adults and apprentices; to establish school banks (*caisses des écoles*); to give advice touching the nomination and promotion of public school teachers, and their rewards and punishments.

Primary inspectors are divided into classes. To be eligible for promotion to a higher class, they must have spent three years in the class next below and must be on the list for advancement made each year by the inspectors general.

4. *By the members of the department council appointed for the purpose.*— These officers inspect only the condition of school buildings, furniture, and supplies, the health and deportment of pupils. They have no authority to touch on the course of study or methods of instruction.

5. *By the mayor and cantonal delegates (délégués cantonaux).*—The inspection of these officers is restricted as explained under 4.

6. *By the inspectresses general and department inspectresses of the écoles maternelles.*— Both classes of officials are appointed by the minister. Inspectresses general must have attained the age of 35 years, with five years' experience in public or private instruction, and hold the certificate of fitness for the inspection of the *écoles maternelles* and *classes enfantines*. Inspectresses general belong to the consultation committee of primary education. Department inspectresses must be 30 years of age, with three years' experience in public or private instruction. They must hold the same certificate of capacity as the inspectresses general. These inspectresses advise the nomination and recall of directors and teachers of *écoles maternelles*. Restricted to these schools their duties correspond in a measure with those of primary inspectors.

An annual examination for the fitness for the inspection of *écoles maternelles* and *classes enfantines* is held before a commission appointed by the minister.

Candidates must be at least 25 years of age. They must have taught at least five years in public schools. They must hold either the *brevet supérieur* (page 43), the *certificat d'aptitude pédagogique* (page 44), or the *certificat d'aptitude à l'enseignement des jeunes filles.*

The examination is both oral and written, including a practical test.

The oral examination embraces hygiene, pedagogy as applied to *écoles maternelles*, school law and school administration, in so far as the same relate to these schools.

The written test consists of two theses, one on some pedagogic subject pertaining to *écoles maternelles*, the other on questions of hygiene relating to these schools.

The practical test is a visit to an *école maternelle* with a verbal report of the same (1887).

7. *From a medical standpoint, by the communal or departmental medical inspectors.*

REGULATION OF INSPECTION.

The inspection of public schools is made in accordance with the decrees of the higher council (page 11).

The inspection of private schools includes morality, hygiene and the obligations imposed by the compulsory education act of March 28, 1882. It touches the course of study and methods of instruction only in so far as the same be contrary to morals, to the constitution and to the laws.

Ministerial decrees regulate the inspection districts, the number of inspectors, their jurisdiction, classification, traveling expenses and promotion.

THIRTEENTH CHAPTER.
TEACHERS' CONFERENCES.

Conferences of teachers for the discussion of questions pertaining to the theory and practice of teaching were established in 1837, but were afterwards abandoned. In 1880 they were reestablished and from that date have been productive of much good. Attendance is compulsory and the expenses of teachers are paid while in attendance. The academy inspector presides at these conferences by right, but, in his absence, the duty devolves on the inspector of primary instruction.

The conferences are held in each canton, though several cantons may unite. The rector decides as to whether male and female teachers are to attend the same conference. Usage varies in this respect. The number, date and place of meeting of these conferences are fixed by academic authority. At the last meeting of each school year, the conference proposes questions for the following year. These are published as soon as possible by the academy inspector. A report of each meeting is sent to the inspector of primary instruction.

In the circular of 1880, relative to these conferences, Jules Ferry, at that time minister of public instruction, wrote: "It is important that our teaching force escape the feeling of isolation which paralyzes the strongest wills. Young or old, normal school graduates or not, teachers must struggle against discouragement and routine. To keep each one in touch nothing is more efficacious than a full body which does not permit any of its members to grow feeble. In associating in these periodic conferences, teachers not only learn to discuss questions of methods and all the details of school organization for which they have a common interest, but they form pleasant relations with their colleagues and increase the points of contact with their superior officers, creating a feeling of good fellowship and a professional spirit which constitute the power and the dignity of the teaching force."

FOURTEENTH CHAPTER.
THE TEACHING FORCE.

No one is permitted to teach in any capacity in a public school unless provided with the certificates required by law.*

GENERAL CERTIFICATES.

The general certificates of capacity for primary instruction are: 1. *T' e brevet élémentaire.* — Candidates must be at least 16 years of age unless a dispensation is granted by the academy inspector. The examination commission is composed of seven members, appointed annually by the rector on the recommendation of the academy inspector. Examinations are held twice a year in each department. Each candidate must present an application written and signed by himself, with his birth certificate, at least fifteen days before the examination. Persons convicted of crime or dishonorable acts, or deprived of all or part of the rights mentioned in article 42 of the penal code, are not admitted to the examination.

The examination involves three series of tests,—

a. An exercise in dictation of about a page in length (the punctuation is not dictated); an exercise in penmanship of one page in *cursive, bâtarde* and *ronde;* an exercise in French composition (letter or simply story, explanation of a proverb, maxim, moral or educational precept); a question in arithmetic and in the metric system with the full solution of a problem (whole numbers, fractions, measure of surfaces and of volumes).

b. The free-hand drawing of a common object of simple form (plan, section, elevation); elementary gymnastic exercises, prescribed for primary schools. The girls substitute a sketch of some common object and specimens of needlework (under the supervision of ladies appointed by the rector for this purpose).

---

* Teachers must now hold State certificates. Before 1881 they were also licensed by ecclesiastics. Time was allowed for eliminating teachers not provided with State licenses.

c. Five oral tests, namely: Reading with explanation, from a collection of extracts in prose and poetry, with questions on the meaning of words, the sequence of ideas and grammatic construction; questions in arithmetic including the metric system; the elements of French history and civics; the geography of France, with exercises on the blackboard; elementary music; elementary notions of the physical and natural sciences. In addition the boys are asked questions pertaining to agriculture. No one is examined on a subsequent series if he or she fail to attain half the maximum credits allowed for the preceding. The oral and written tests should not in any case go beyond the mean of the courses of study of the highest class in the primary schools. The fee for the examination is two dollars. Normal school pupils are exempt. Rejected candidates may present themselves at the next examination (1887, 1888, 1889).

2. *The brevet supérieur.*— Candidates must hold the *brevet élémentaire.* They must be at least 18 years of age unless a dispensation is granted by the academy inspector. The examining commission is composed of at least seven members, appointed annually by the rector, on the recommendation of the academy inspectors. Examinations are held twice a year in each depart. ment. Candidates must present the *brevet élémentaire*, an application in their own handwriting and signature, and birth certificate, at least fifteen days before the examination. Persons convicted of crime or dishonorable acts or deprived of all or part of the rights mentioned in article 42 of the penal code are not admitted to the examination.

The examination comprises oral and written tests, all of which must be borne at the same session.

The written tests are,—

a. A composition including a question in arithmetic, and one on the physical and natural sciences with the most common applications to hygiene, industry, agriculture and horticulture. The male candidates have in addition a question involving practical operations in geometry. They are permitted to use a table of logarithms;

b. A French composition (literature or *morale*);

c. An exercise in drawing from a model;

d. A composition in modern languages (English, German, Italian, Spanish, or Arabic, in France and Algeria; Greek or Turkish, before the commission at Constantinople), consisting of an easy theme, with lexicon.

The oral tests are,—

a. Questions on education and morals;

b. The French language: Reading with explanation from a French author on the list prepared once in three years by the minister and published a year in advance; questions in literary history, limited to the principal authors of the 16th, 17th, 18th and 19th centuries;

c. Questions on memorable epochs, great names, essential facts in general history and in the history of France, principally in modern times;

d. Questions on the geography of France, and notions of general geography.

e. Arithmetic, with practical applications; book-keeping, and, for the men alone, an elementary knowledge of geometric and algebraic calculations, land surveying and leveling.

f. Notions of physics, chemistry and natural history, and, for the males alone, an elementary knowledge of agriculture and horticulture.

g. Translation at sight of about twenty lines from an easy English, German, Italian, Spanish or Arabic text at the choice of the candidate. Greek or Turkish may be substituted before the commission at Constantinople. The written and oral tests of the *brevet supérieur* ought not to exceed in difficulty the mean of the normal school courses of study. The fee for the examination is four dollars. Normal school pupils are exempt. Rejected candidates may present themselves at the next examination (1887, 1888, 1889).

3. The *certificat d'aptitude pédagogique.*—Candidates must be 21 years of age. They must hold at least the *brevet élémentaire.* They must have had an experience of at least two years in public or private schools. The time passed at a normal school as pupil-teacher after 18 years of age for the males and 17 years for the females is allowed to count toward the experience required. Dispensations may be granted by the minister on the recommendation of the department council. An annual examination is held in each department before a commission of at least ten members, appointed by the rector on the recommendation of the academy inspector. Candidates must apply at least fifteen days in advance, presenting an application in their own handwriting and with their own signature; the birth certificate; the *brevet élémentaire* or the *brevet supérieur.* The examination is both written and oral, including a practical test.

The written examination consists of a thesis on some elementary educational topic, composed during the last week of the long vacation under the supervision of the primary inspector, and corrected by the commission.

The practical test consists of three hours' work in the school or class of the applicant. A sub-commission, composed of at least three members, including a primary inspector and a male teacher (for the males) and a female teacher (for the females) is appointed by the academy inspector for the purpose of supervising the test. The female may take this test in an *école maternelle*, but in this case the certificate authorizes her to teach only as *titulaire* in these schools. Private teachers are permitted to undergo this test either in their own class or in a public school.

The oral test which is taken before the whole commission consists of criticism of books of monthly tasks (*cahiers de devoirs mensuels*); questions relating to the other tests and involving the keeping and direction of elementary schools or *écoles maternelles* and questions on practical pedagogy (1887, 1888).

4. *Certificate as professor of the upper primary schools.*—The qualifications are the same as those for the certificate of professor in the primary normal schools for males and females (1887).

5. *Certificate as professor of the primary normal schools for males and females.*—There are two kinds of certificates, one for the arts and one for the sciences. Two commissions are named by the minister annually, one for the sciences and one for the arts. Each commission is composed of at least five members. To these are added, for the females, two directresses or professors of normal schools for females. Special examinations may also be appointed. Candidates must register one month before the opening of the session. They must be at least 21 years of age and must specify where they have lived and what positions they have held. They must hold the *brevet supérieur* or a bachelor's degree or (the females) a diploma from a secondary school. They must have had at least two years' experience in public or private schools.

The tests are written, oral and practical.

The written tests comprise, for the arts,—

A theme on a literary or grammatic subject; an historic and geographic essay; a theme on *morale* or psychology as applied to education; a composition in English or German, theme and version. For the sciences, the written examination comprises a mathematic exercise; questions in physics, chemistry and the natural sciences; an exercise in geometric and ornamental drawing; a theme on *morale* or education. The subjects are chosen from the courses of study in the primary normal schools.

The oral and practical proofs comprise, for the arts, a lesson on some subject chosen by lot, followed by interrogations; the reading of a passage from a French classic, with explanation; the correction of a task of a pupil-teacher; the explanation at sight of a German or English text, chosen from the official list of authors. The test for the sciences consists of a lesson on a subject chosen by lot (mathematics or physical and natural sciences); an exercise on some other subject included in the course of study, which may comprise the correction of a task of a pupil-teacher; a physical or chemical experiment and a practical lesson in natural history, the subject to be drawn by lot.

SPECIAL CERTIFICATES.

The special certificates for particular lines of primary work are,—

1. *Certificate as teacher of modern languages.*— Candidates must have attained the age of 21 years. They must have had two years' experience in public or private primary or secondary schools, or two years' residence in a foreign country. The males must hold the *brevet supérieur* or one of the three bachelors' degrees; the females the *brevet supérieur* or the diploma received on graduation from a secondary school for girls. The examination is held before a commission, named annually by the minister and sitting at Paris.

Candidates must specify the language in which they desire to be examined (German, English, Italian, Spanish, Arabic); the diplomas and certificates which they possess; the places where they have resided, and the positions they have held.

The examination is both written and oral.

The written examination comprises a version; a theme; a simple composition in the foreign language (letter or story, explanation of a proverb, maxim, moral or educational precept); an essay in French touching the method of teaching modern languages. The use of the dictionary is not authorized.

The oral examination includes the reading and translation of a page of moderate difficulty, selected from the list of authors prescribed for the year, with definitions of words and grammatic construction; a conversational exercise, in the foreign tongue, on the page read; the translation at sight of a French prose author; question on methods of teaching modern languages (1887).

2. *Certificate as teacher of manual training.*— Candidates should be 21 years of age. The males should hold the *brevet supérieur*, the degree of bachelor of science or bachelor of special secondary

Alberto   *Elementaire*
                Anglais

I am a boy
thou art a lady
He is a mother
we are six brothers
you are five sisters
they are ten girls

I was a uncle
thou wast a sister
He was a niece
we were six cousins
you were eleven nephews
they were five aunt
I shall be a husband
Thou will be a wife
He will be a mother
we shall be six fathers
you will be eleven brothers
they will be six cousins

English Exercise by French Boy Seven Years of Age.

The exercise here given was selected at a recitation in the elementary course of one of the special Parisian schools in which English is taught. It seems to illustrate the fact that gender in English seems as difficult to French as gender in French to English pupils.

instruction.* The females should hold the *brevet supérieur* or the diploma received on graduation from a secondary school for girls.

The examination is held by two commissions, one for males, the other for females.

These commissions are named each year by the minister, and sit at Paris.

Candidates should register one month in advance, submitting a biographic sketch of the six years preceding the examination, and proving the possession of the requisite certificates.

The males must submit,—

a. A geometric drawing at a fixed scale of an object in relief, or a drawing involving an elementary problem in descriptive geometry (line and plane, intersection of geometric solids in simple cases — prisms, pyramids, cylinders, cones and spheres, shading);

b. A written composition on some pedagogic subject related to manual instruction;

c. A test in modeling from an easy model;

d. A piece in iron or wood made from a working drawing;

e. A simple exercise in turning and sculpturing after a model;

f. An explanation, in the form of a lesson of fifteen minutes, of a subject drawn by lot from matters which should be commented on by the teacher before every exercise in manual training, such as the tools, the material, the plan and the rational execution of the task. Candidates are allowed one-half hour for preparation.

The females must submit,—

a. A composition on some question in domestic economy;

b. An ornamental design for needlework;

c. A practical test, including one or more exercises from the courses of study in manual training for girls in the normal and upper primary schools;

d. An explanation, in the form of a fifteen minute lesson, of a subject included in the courses of study of the schools last mentioned in domestic economy and needlework. One-half hour is allowed for preparation.

The candidates may ask for the following additional tests:

a. Drawing from an ornament in relief;

b. A blackboard exercise of ten minutes, after twenty minutes' preparation, consisting of a lesson on the representation at sight of some common object in perspective. Certificates of candidates

---

*In France the degrees bachelor of arts and bachelor of science may be secured at 16 years of age. They are not as advanced as our own bachelors' degrees, to which the *diplome de licencié es lettres* and the *diplome de licencié es sciences* more nearly correspond.

sustaining these complementary tests authorize the teaching of imitative drawing (*dessin d' imitation*) in the upper primary schools (1887, 1891).

3. *Certificate as teacher of drawing* (*dessin d' imitation et dessin géométrique*).—An annual examination is held at Paris by a commission named by the minister. The candidates must be 18 years of age and must register one month in advance. The examination comprises three series of tests — written and graphic, oral, pedagogic.

The written and graphic tests include:

a. Representation in perspective of a simple object, such as a geometric solid, fragment of architecture, simple vase, etc. The candidate must give on the same sheet a geometric plan and elevation, and, if necessary, a section of the object represented, the whole with dimensions and drawn to a fixed scale.

b. A simple theme;

c. The drawing at sight of an ornament in relief — foliage, rosette, capital;

d. The drawing of a head after the antique.

The oral tests comprise an examination on projections in general, on geometric representation and the drawing in perspective of simple objects; elementary questions on historic art with drawing on blackboard; questions on the structure and proportions of the human body and anatomy in general.

The pedagogic tests comprise the correction of one of the ornamental drawings made at the examination; the correction of a drawing of a head; a lesson on the blackboard on a subject included in the course of instruction in geometric drawing at the normal and upper primary schools (1887).

4. *Certificate as teacher of singing.*—An annual examination is held before a commission at Paris, named by the minister. Candidates must be 18 years of age and must register at least fifteen days before the examination.

There are two series of tests.

The first series includes,—

a. A theme on some question of musical instruction found in the normal school courses of study;

b. An exercise in musical dictation;

c. An exercise in construction and harmonization;

The second series includes,—

a. Reading at sight a lesson in *solfège* in the key of *sol* and in the key of *fa*;

b. Singing of a melody with words, chosen by the candidate;

c. Performance of an air by heart, with words and without accompaniment, chosen by the candidate;

d. Performance at sight of a simple accompaniment on the piano, which is to be transposed at once into the key indicated by the jury;

e. Questions on the theory of music;

f. Notions of the history of music;

Knowledge of the principal masterpieces of choral music;

g. A theoretic and practical lesson by the candidate on the blackboard (1887).

5. *Certificate as teacher of gymnastics.*— An annual examination is held before a commission which is named by the rector and which sits at Paris.

Candidates must register at least fifteen days before the examination, and must state where they have resided, what positions they have occupied, and what certificates they hold.

The examination comprises oral and practical tests.

The oral examination embraces questions on those sciences which find a direct application in the study of gymnastics (according to ministerial decree).

The practical examination includes the performance of five gymnastic exercises from among those prescribed in the manual published by the ministry; the direction of the gymnastic exercises of a group of pupils (1887, 1888, 1891).

6. *Certificate as teacher of needlework.*— The examination is held before a commission in each department. Applicants must register at least eight days before the examination. They must be 18 years of age and, with their application in their own handwriting and signature, they must submit their birth certificate.

The needlework which candidates are to execute is chosen from the courses of study in the middle and upper classes of the lower primary schools (1887).

7. *Certificate as teacher of military exercises.*— The examination is held before a commission in each department. Candidates should register eight days in advance. They should be 18 years of age, and with the application written in their own hand and signed, they should submit their birth certificate; a certificate of the military authorities that they have served in the active army, and have merited the certificate of good conduct.

Candidates direct the military exercises of a group of pupils as indicated by the commission in accordance with the program of the lower primary schools (1887).

8. *Certificate as teacher of agriculture.*—Candidates should hold the *brevet supérieur* and the *certificat d'aptitude pédagogique*, and should have been for one year in a State agricultural school. Dispensations may be granted by the minister on the recommendation of the rector.

The possession of the professor's certificate for the normal schools and for the upper primary schools does away with the necessity of holding the *certificat d'aptitude pédagogique.*

The examination includes oral, written and practical tests.

The written tests consist of a composition on a subject included in the course of study in agriculture and horticulture in the upper primary schools. Candidates are forbidden to use any book or note.

The oral tests consist of an explanation, after preparation with closed doors, of a subject taken from the course of study of upper primary schools in agriculture and horticulture; of questions on the physical and natural sciences in their relations to agriculture.

The practical proofs are two in number. The first is in connection with agricultural experiments or land improvements. It embraces the composition of the soil, the proper manures, the manner of using, the seed to sow, the variety of plants to cultivate, the manner of cultivation, the feeding of live stock, the poultry, etc. The second takes place in a garden. It relates to the operations of grafting and pruning, to the multiplication of fruit trees, to market-gardening, apiculture, etc. In the course of these tests, the candidates are to respond to questions of the jury, particularly concerning products of the neighborhood (1891).

9. *Certificate as director of normal school.* The qualifications are the same as those for an inspector of primary schools and are given in the chapter on inspection.

CLASSES OF TEACHERS.—PENALTIES AND RECOMPENSES.

Male and female teachers are divided into two classes, called *stagiaires* and *titulaires.*

No one can be appointed *instituteur titulaire* if he has not had at least two years' experience in a public or private school, if he is not provided with the *certificat d'aptitude pédagogique*, and if he has not been placed on the list prepared by the department council.

The time passed at the normal school after 18 for the males and 17 for the females is allowed in reckoning the two years.

Dispensations may be granted by the minister on the recommendation of the department council.

The *titulaires* in charge of a school with more than two classes take the name *directeur* or *directrice* of lower primary schools.

The number of assistants in schools with several classes is determined by the department council. These assistants are either *stagiaires* or *titulaires*. Assistants in upper primary schools must be 21 years of age and hold the *brevet supérieur*. If provided with the certificate of capacity for a professorship in normal schools, they assume the title professor.

All public school teachers are shut out from the commercial and industrial professions, and from administrative duties. They are forbidden to hold employments in connection with religious services. They may exercise the duties of mayoralty-secretary, with the authorization of the department council.

Instituteurs stagiaires teach under appointment of the academy inspector. This appointment may be revoked by the academy inspector for cause shown by the primary inspector.

The *stagiaires* are subject to the same disciplines as the *titulaires*, excepting revocation.

The department council prepares annually a list of all teachers eligible for promotion to the rank of *titulaires* as assistants in or in charge of a school.

The appointment of *instituteurs titulaires* is made by the prefect, with the authority of the minister and on the proposition of the academy inspector.

Directors, directresses and professors of upper primary schools are appointed by the minister. They should hold the certificate of fitness for a professorship in the normal schools.

Assistant teachers holding the *brevet supérieur*, and special teachers, are appointed by the prefect on the recommendation of the academy inspector.

Directors and directresses of schools of manual training are appointed by the minister according to the conditions of the law of December 11, 1880, and the decree of March 17, 1888.

Change of residence of *titulaires* for the needs of the service is pronounced by the prefect on the recommendation of the academy inspector. Change of residence of *stagiaires* is pronounced by the academy inspector.

The disciplines applicable to the public primary teaching force are reprimand, censure, revocation, suspension for a period not exceeding five years, expulsion.

The reprimand is pronounced by the academy inspector. The censure is given by the academy inspector on cause shown by the department council. It may be inserted in the official bulletin.

The revocation is pronounced by the prefect on the proposition of the academy inspector and for cause shown by the department council. An appeal may be made to the minister. Temporary suspension and absolute expulsion are pronounced by a decree of the department council.

An appeal may be made to the higher council.

In serious and urgent cases the academy inspector may suspend a teacher while the investigation is pending, but said teacher does not forfeit his salary for the period.

Public primary school teachers may receive honorable mention, bronze and silver medals.

One silver medal may be given annually for each group of 300 teachers, and one for each fraction exceeding 150.

One bronze medal may be given for each group of 150 teachers.

One honorable mention may be pronounced for each 100 teachers.

No one can obtain honorable mention who has not at least five years' experience as *titulaire*.

No one can obtain the bronze medal unless he received honorable mention at least two years before.

No one can obtain the silver medal unless he received the bronze medal at least two years before.

Retired teachers may be given the title honorary, if they have had twenty-five years' active service and hold at least the bronze medal. They are permitted to take part in the pedagogic conferences of their cantons.

FIFTEENTH CHAPTER.
COMPULSORY EDUCATION.

Primary instruction comprises:
Morals and civics;
Reading and writing;
The French language and the elements of French literature;
Geography, particularly that of France;
History, particularly French history up to our own day;
Common notions of law and of political economy;
The elements of the natural sciences, physics and mathematics; their applications to agriculture, hygiene, the industrial arts; manual training and use of tools of the principal trades;
The elements of drawing, modeling and music;
Gymnastics;

Military exercises, for the boys;
Needlework, for the girls.

Primary instruction is obligatory for children of both sexes from 6 to 13 years of age. It may be given in primary or secondary schools, in public or private schools or in the family (by the father or by any person whom he may choose).

A special regulation determines the means of assuring primary instruction to deaf-mutes and to the blind.

Public primary schools are to be closed one day in each week in addition to Sunday, that parents may give their children religious instruction outside the school buildings, if they desire to do so. Religious instruction may not be given in the school buildings or their dependencies.

COMMISSIONS SCOLAIRES.

In each commune there is a school committee (*commission scolaire*), which supervises and encourages the frequentation of the schools. It is composed of the mayor or of an assistant delegated by him, as president; of one of the cantonal delegates and, in communes comprising several cantons, of as many delegates as there are cantons, appointed by the academy inspector; of members designated by the municipal council in number not exceeding one-third the members of the council. In case the municipal council fail to nominate these members, they are appointed by the prefect.

At Paris and at Lyons there is a *commission scolaire* for each municipal *arrondissement*, presided over by the mayor or by an assistant designated by him. It is composed of one of the cantonal delegates appointed by the academy inspector, and of from three to seven members for each *arrondissement*, designated by the municipal council.

The terms of members appointed by the municipal council expire with the election of a new council.

The primary inspector is a member of all *commissions scolaires* in his district.

The law of April 5, 1884, determines the question of eligibility to membership in a *commission scolaire*.

The *commission scolaire* meets at least once in three months on the call of the president or of the primary inspector. A majority of the members constitute a quorum for the transaction of business; but if after two calls there is not a quorum, the *commission scolaire* may transact the special business for which it was convened provided the mayor or the assistant who takes his place, the primary inspector and the cantonal delegate are present.

Unexcused absence at three consecutive meetings works forfeiture of membership.

A copy of the proceedings of the *commission scolaire* is to be forwarded by the president to the primary inspector within three days after the meeting.

The *commission scolaire* may not interfere with matters and methods of instruction.

The primary inspector, parents or guardians may appeal from decisions of *commissions scolaires*. The appeal, in the form of a simple letter, is to be addressed within six days, to the prefect and to the persons interested. It may be referred to the department council as a court of last resort. Parents or guardians may be represented by attorneys before the department council.

The sessions of the department councils and of *commissions scolaires* are not public.

CERTIFICATE OF PRIMARY STUDIES.

A certificate of primary studies (*certificat d'études primaires*) is awarded to those children who at the age of 11 years and upward complete successfully the public examination prescribed by law. Holders of this certificate are freed from the obligation to attend school.

Cantonal commissions are appointed by the rectors, on the proposition of the academy inspectors, to judge of the fitness of candidates for the certificate of primary studies. These commissions meet annually on the call of the academy inspector. The primary inspector is the presiding officer. In the examination of girls, some members of the commission must be women.

At the time prescribed by the academy inspector, each teacher prepares a list of the candidates in his school, with name, date and place of birth, residence of the family and signature of each candidate.

Parents whose children do not attend school must furnish the same information.

The list is certified by the mayor, and transmitted to the primary inspector.

No candidate may be admitted who is under 11 years of age at the date of the examination.

The examination is both written and oral.

The written tests are under the supervision of the members of the commission, and are private.

They include:

1. An exercise in dictation of not more than fifteen lines; the end of each sentence is indicated;

9ᵉ ARRONDISSEMENT

École de Garçons
Rue Blanche

RÉPUBLIQUE FRANÇAISE
LIBERTÉ, ÉGALITÉ, FRATERNITÉ

Ville de Paris

Devoir dicté le 12 Mars 1887

Dedieu
cours moyen
10 ans

Il existe un très beau livre qui a pour titre : les aventures de Télémaque, fils d'Ulysse. C'est l'histoire d'un jeune prince Grec qui voyage à la recherche de son père, et dont la sagesse triomphe d'un grand nombre d'obstacles et de dangers. Ce livre excellent, rempli d'une morale admirable, a été composé pour l'éducation du petit fils de Louis XIV par un homme célèbre, grand écrivain et vertueux prélat, Fénelon, archevêque de Cambrai. Vous apprendrez, au sud-est du département du Nord, cette ville de Cambrai, illustrée par le séjour qu'il y a fait.

Dedieu

Exercise in Dictation by French Boy Ten Years of Age.

The selection for this exercise was chosen by me and was dictated to the class by the teacher, who indicated punctuation. The time allowed was too short for careful and neat work. The other specimens are about the same. This work was done in the middle course of a public elementary school in Paris.

2. Two questions in arithmetic, including the metric system;

3. A simple composition (story, letter, etc.).

Girls are to execute a task in needlework under the supervision of a woman appointed for the purpose.

The time and credits allotted to each test are given in the following table:

TEST.	Time.	Credits.
Orthography*.		10
Penmanship		10
Arithmetic	1 hour	10
Composition	1 hour	10
Needlework	1 hour	10

Only those candidates are admitted to the oral examination who succeed in obtaining at least 50 per cent of the total number of credits. Zero in any one test involves rejection.

The oral tests are public. They take place before a special commission under the primary inspector as presiding officer.

They include:

Reading with explanation, and the recitation of a selection chosen from a list presented by the candidate;

Questions in history and geography.

Ten credits are allotted to each test. The oral examination is not to exceed fifteen minutes in length for each candidate.

No one receives a certificate of primary studies who fails to obtain 50 per cent of the total number of credits allotted to the written and oral examinations.

On demand of candidates, linear drawing and agriculture may be included in the examination.

Certificates mention complementary subjects in which candidates have attained 50 per cent.

A report of the examination is forwarded to the academy inspector who satisfies himself as to the regularity of the proceedings and then issues certificates to successful candidates.

In 1882, 91,153 certificates of primary studies were issued; in 1887, the corresponding number reported was 144,046.

---

* The text is read aloud, dictated, then reread, and five minutes are allowed candidates for corrections.

OTHER PROVISIONS OF THE COMPULSORY EDUCATION LAW.

The father or guardian of a child subject to the compulsory education law must give the mayor of the commune notice at least fifteen days before the opening of the term whether the child is to receive instruction in the family, in a public or private school, indicating the school.

Families living near several public schools may choose between these schools, whether they are situated in their commune or not, provided the number of pupils does not exceed the maximum authorized by the regulations. In cases of dispute, the department council is the final court of appeal.

The mayor prepares annually, with the assistance of the *commission scolaire*, a list of all the children from 6 to 13 years of age, and advises parents and guardians of the date of the opening of the term.

In case the parents or guardians fail to give notice fifteen days before the opening of the term, the child is enrolled by the mayor in one of the public schools and a notice is sent to the parents or guardian.

Eight days before the opening of the term, the mayor submits to the directors of public and private schools a list of the children who ought to attend. A copy of this list is sent to the primary inspector.

When a child leaves school, the parents or guardians must give notice immediately to the mayor, indicating how the child is to receive instruction in the future.

Parents or guardians must inform the school-director of the reasons for temporary absences.

School-directors must keep a register, showing for each class the attendance of pupils registered. At the end of each month they must send an abstract of this register to the mayor, indicating the number of absences and the reasons therefor.

Excuses for absence are submitted to the *commission scolaire*. The only excuses deemed sufficient are sickness of the child, death of a member of the family, detentions resulting from imperfect communications, accidental in character. Exceptional circumstances meet due consideration before the commission.

Every director of a private school who fails to conform to the preceding prescriptions is reported by the commission and the primary inspector to the department council. The council may then pronounce the following punishments.

a. Warning; *b.* Censure; *c.* Suspension for a month at the most, and, in case of repetition of the offense, for three months at most.

When a child shall have been absent four times in one month, during at least one-half day, without justification by the **commission**,

Die Roßkastanie.

Die Roßkastanie ist ein 20—30 m hoher Baum mit geradem dicken Stamme und großer dichter Krone. Die Blätter sind gegenständig und 7zählig gefingert. Die Blättchen sind ungleich groß. Die zwei äußeren Blättchen sind am kleinsten und das obere ist am größten. Die Blättchen sind länglich [illegible] und kahl und gezähnt. Sie haben eine starke Mittelrippe. Die Blüten der Roßkastanie bilden aufrechtstehende Pyrami.

[illegible]
10 Jahre alt.

Exercise in Reproduction by German Boy Ten Years of Age.

The exercise here given for comparison is one of the best of the specimens prepared during my visit at a public elementary school in Burtscheid near Aix-la-Chapelle, though those from a majority of the class are nearly as good.

the father or guardian is asked at least three days in advance to appear before the commission at the mayoralty. He is there reminded of the duty imposed by the law.

In case of repetition of the offense within a twelvemonth, the child is posted for fifteen days or one month at the entrance to the mayoralty, with the full name and standing of the person responsible and with an indication of the charge.

In case of a second repetition of the offense, the commission or the primary inspector lodge a complaint with the police justice, who pronounces sentences according to articles 479, 480 sq. of the penal code. Article 463 of the same code is applicable. The *commission scolaire* may grant children living with parents or guardians, on reasonable demand, a dispensation of three months annually, exclusive of vacations. If the dispensation exceed fifteen days the primary inspector must approve.

These dispositions are not applicable to children accompanying their parents or guardians when absenting themselves temporarily from the commune. In this case a verbal or written notice to the mayor suffices. No child under 12 can be employed industrially unless in actual attendance on a public or private school. Every child employed industrially who is under 12 years of age must attend school during leisure hours. He must receive daily at least two hours' instruction, if a special school is attached to the industrial establishment. A record of attendance is kept by the teacher and transmitted weekly to the patron. No child under 15 is permitted to work more than six hours a day, unless he produces a certificate from the teacher or primary inspector, legalized by the mayor, that he has received elementary primary instruction.

The *commission scolaire*, with the approval of the department council, may dispense children employed industrially and having attained the age of apprenticeship from one of the two classes of the day. The same dispensation may be granted to children employed outside of their families in agriculture.

Children receiving instruction in the family must pass each year, beginning with the end of the second year of the compulsory period, an examination on the work done in public schools by pupils of their age. The forms and programs of these examinations are determined by ministerial decrees, rendered in higher council (*conseil supérieur*).

The examining committee is composed of the primary inspector or his delegate, as chairman; a cantonal delegate; a person holding a university diploma or brevet of capacity. The judges are chosen by the academy inspector.

If the examination of the child is unsatisfactory and an excuse is not admitted by the committee, the parents or guardians must send the child, within eight days of the notification, to a public or private school, and inform the mayor what school has been chosen. In case this is not done by the parent or guardian, it will be done through the mayoralty.

School *caisses*, designed to encourage and facilitate the frequentation of schools by recompensing the studious and assisting the diligent, are established in each commune (Law of April 10, 1867).

The revenues of these *caisses* depend on voluntary subscriptions, grants from the commune, the department and the State. They may also be authorized by prefects to receive gifts and legacies.

In subsidized communes where the value of the *centime* does not exceed thirty francs, the *caisse* is entitled, on the credit opened for this purpose at the ministry of public instruction, to a grant equal at least to the total of the communal grants.

The distribution of succor is made through the *commission scolaire*. Ministerial decrees, given on demand of academy inspectors and department councils, fix each year the communes in which, owing to insufficient school accommodations, the provisions of the Compulsory Education Act can not be strictly enforced. The minister reports these communes annually to the *chambres*.

An examination of the statistics relating to compulsory education shows that France has no reason to blush as regards her school accommodations. Would that we were able to say the same for New York. As we think, however, of the thousands of children who are shut out of school entirely owing to the lack of accommodations, we are far from satisfied with the results of our school work.*

SIXTEENTH CHAPTER.

EXPENSES OF PUBLIC PRIMARY INSTRUCTION AND SALARIES.

LAW OF JULY 19, 1889.

Art. 1.— The ordinary expenses of public primary instruction are paid by the State, the departments and the communes.

Art. 2.— *The State pays:*

a. The salaries of employés in public elementary schools and *écoles maternelles;*

---

* We should have statistics showing the number of children in New York between 6 and 13 years of age, and the registration and attendance of these children in elementary schools. Comparisons based on these figures would afford a strong argument for the enactment of an effective compulsory education law.

b. The salaries of employés in upper primary schools and manual training schools;
c. The supplements referred to in articles 8 and 9;
d. The salaries of employés in normal schools;
e. The salaries of administrative and supervising officers;
f. Traveling expenses of supervising officers;
g. The maintenance of students in normal schools and other expenses of these schools not specially provided for;
h. The allowance (twenty dollars) for the silver medal.

Art. 3.— *The departments pay :*
a. The allowance of at least forty dollars to primary inspectors;
b. The maintenance of normal school buildings;
c. The maintenance of the furniture and teaching supplies of normal schools;
d. The rent and maintenance of the office and furniture for the department service of public instruction;
e. The office expenses of the academy inspector;
f. The cost of books and pamphlets used by the cantonal delegations and the academic administration;
g. The allowances made to foremen, assistants and workmen charged by the departments with agricultural, commercial or industrial instruction in all primary schools and in technical schools ruled by the law of December 11, 1880.

Art. 4.—*The communes pay :*
a. The allowance for lodgings referred to in article 12.
b. The maintenance and location of primary school buildings; the lodgings of teachers or the allowances therefor;
c. The cost of heating and lighting the primary schools;
d. The wages of servants in public *écoles maternelles*, and (if there be any) in other public primary schools;
e. The acquisition, maintenance and replacement of school furniture and teaching supplies;
f. The cost of registers, books and pamphlets used in the schools;
g. The allowances made to foremen, assistants and workmen charged by the communes with agricultural, commercial or industrial instruction in primary schools of all grades and in technical schools ruled by the law of December 11, 1880.

Art. 5.—Upper primary schools and complementary courses cease to be maintained by the State if the total number of pupils for three consecutive years is less than fifteen for each year of the course in upper primary schools, and twelve for each year of the course in the *cours complémentaires.*

SALARIES.
CITATIONS FROM THE LAW OF JULY 19, 1889.

Art. 6. — Male and female teachers are divided into *stagiaires* and *titulaires*.*

Art. 7. — The *titulaires* are divided into five classes. The salaries are fixed as follows:

	Males.	Females.
Fifth class	$200	$200
Fourth class	240	240
Third class	300	280
Second class	360	300
First class	400	320

Art. 8. — *Titulaires* in charge of a school with more than two classes receive a supplement of forty dollars, which is increased to eighty dollars if the school have more than four classes.

Art. 9. — In schools with a complementary course, the teacher in charge of the same receives a supplement of forty dollars.

Art. 10. — In addition to salary, *titulaires* are entitled to lodgings or to an allowance therefor, as set forth under article 12.

Art. 11. — *Stagiaires*, male and female, receive a salary of $160 and lodgings, or an allowance therefor, as set forth under article 12.

Art. 12. — The allowance for lodgings for teachers referred to in articles 8, 9, 14 and 15 is determined according to the following table:

Close population of locality.	Allowance.
Less than 1,000, if *chefs-lieux*; 1,000 to 3,000, if not	$20
3,001 to 9,000	40
9,001 to 12,000	60
12,001 to 18,000	80
18,001 to 35,000	100
35,001 to 60,000	120
60,001 to 100,000	140
Above 100,000	160
In the city of Paris	400

For all other *titulaires* the allowances are one-half the above figures. The allowances of *stagiaires* are one-quarter the above figures.

---

* *Stagiaires* are on probation and are appointed by the academy inspectors. They constitute about 20 per cent of the teaching force. *Titulaires* are in full standing and are appointed by the prefects from lists prepared by the department councils.

In cities with more than 100,000 inhabitants and in the communes of the department of the Seine, the allowance may be increased. *

Art. 13.—Directors, directresses and assistants in upper primary schools; directors and professors of normal schools; normal school stewards and primary inspectors are divided into five classes.

Art. 14.—The salaries of directors and directresses of upper primary schools are fixed as follows:

Fifth class	$360
Fourth class	400
Third class	440
Second class	500
First class	560

They receive in addition lodgings or the allowance therefor as provided in article 12.

Art. 15.—The salaries of assistants in upper primary schools are fixed as follows:

Fifth class	$220
Fourth class	260
Third class	320
Second class	380
First class	420

In addition lodgings or allowance therefor as set forth in article 12.

Special teachers receive an allowance of from ten dollars to twenty dollars a year for each hour of instruction per week.

Art. 16.—In the national schools of upper primary and technical instruction, the salaries of each class are $100 more than those paid in normal schools for males.

Art. 17.—The salaries of directors and directresses of normal schools are fixed as follows:

	Directors.	Directresses.
Fifth class	$700	$600
Fourth class	800	700
Third class	900	800
Second class	1,000	900
First class	1,100	1,000

In Paris the salary of the director is from $1,400 to $2,000; of the directress, from $1,200 to $1,800.

*October 25, 1891, the educational congress (Congrès de la ligue de l'enseignement) adopted resolutions demanding a return to the scale of salaries in force previous to 1889, and an equal allowance for lodgings for all teachers, after January 1, 1892.

Art. 18.—The salaries of normal school professors are fixed as follows:

	Males.	Females.
Fifth class	$480	$440
Fourth class	520	480
Third class	560	520
Second class	620	560
First class	680	600

Male and female teachers not holding the certificate of capacity for a professorship receive salaries of $400 and $360 respectively.

All salaries given above are eighty dollars less if teachers are odged and fed in the schools.

Art. 19.— Salaries of teachers and other employés in advanced normal schools (*écoles normales supérieures d'enseignement primaire*) are fixed by a special regulation.

Art. 20.— Directors, directresses and assistants in upper primary schools, holding the certificate of capacity for a professorship in normal schools, receive an allowance of $100.

Art. 21.— In normal schools with less than sixty students, the duties of steward are confided to one of the teachers, who receives an allowance of $100 therefor.

In normal schools with more than sixty students, the stewards give no instruction save in writing and book-keeping. Their salaries are fixed as follows:

Fifth class	$360
Fourth class	400
Third class	440
Second class	500
First class	500

In addition, they are entitled to lodgings.

Art. 22.— The salaries of primary inspectors are fixed as follows:

Fifth class	$600
Fourth class	700
Third class	800
Second class	900
First class	1,000

In the department of the Seine, the salaries are $1,200, $1,300, $1,400, $1,500 and $1,600.

Primary inspectresses may be named under the same conditions and in the same form as the inspectors.

Art. 23.— In addition to the salaries as above, primary inspectors are entitled to a department allowance of at least forty dollars.

Art. 24.— Promotion is from class to class. Teachers of the fifth and fourth classes may not be promoted to a higher class without an experience of five years in the class to which they belong.

Promotion to the second and first class requires the *brevet supérieur*, and at least three years' experience in the class next below.

OBSERVATIONS.

It is interesting to note the approximate equalization of wages paid male and female teachers. In many grades of work, as will be seen, there is absolutely no distinction made between male and female teachers.

The table of allowances made for lodgings illustrates the fact that city life is more expensive than country life.

SEVENTEENTH CHAPTER.
MILITARY SERVICE.*
EXTRACTS FROM THE LAW OF JULY 19, 1889.

Art. 1.— Every Frenchman is subject to military service.

Art. 23.— The following persons are dismissed in times of peace after one year's military service:

Young men under bonds to serve ten years in public instruction, in national institutions for the deaf and dumb or blind.

Lay teachers, novices and members of religious bodies devoted to instruction which is of public utility, and who are under bonds to serve ten years in the French schools of the Orient and of Africa.

All persons above enumerated are recalled for four weeks during the year preceding their passage to the reserve of the active army; They then follow the lot of the class to which they belong.

Art. 24.— Young men who do not succeed in finding an employment as teachers during the year following their year of military service, or who cease to be employed at the expiration of the time; young men who, in the year of military service, have failed to meet the conditions established by the Minister of War must serve the two years from which they have been exempted.

---

* We publish only certain extracts relative to persons connected with primary instruction.

Art. 25.—When the causes for which exemption have been made cease to operate, the young men who have been exempted become subject to all the obligations of the class to which they belong.

They may marry without authorization.

Art. 26.—A list of the young men of each department, exempted under the law, is published in the *Bulletin administratif,* and the names of persons exempted in each commune are posted at the entrance to the mayoralty. In case of war, they are summoned to march with the men of their class.

Art. 51.—In case of mobilization, only those specified in official lists are freed from immediate military service.

OBSERVATIONS.

American visitors to French schools for boys will note at once the atmosphere of war by which they are surrounded.

The target practice and drill of the school battalions, and the military exercises in general, may aid the physical development of the pupils, but the earnestness of the instruction suggests unpleasant possibilities.

EIGHTEENTH CHAPTER.
PENSIONS.*

Primary inspectors; directresses and assistants in normal schools; communal teachers and assistants; communal directresses of *salles d' asile* (*écoles maternelles* and *classes enfantines*) are among the employés entitled to pensions under the law of June 9, 1853.

The amount of the pension is not to be less than $120 for a male teacher and $100 for a female teacher. This minimum does not apply to those pensioned exceptionally owing to infirmities.

The amount of the pension is based on the mean of the salary and emoluments for the six years during which these figures were the greatest (Law of August 17, 1876). It is never to exceed three-quarters of the average salary of those years.

The right to a pension is acquired at 60 years of age and after thirty years' service. Persons connected with primary instruction acquire this right at 55 years of age and after twenty-five years' service, provided they have passed fifteen years in what is called the *partie active.*

---

* Civil pensions and the law of 1889 relative to salaries have been among the subjects of general discussion in France in 1891. Several projects have been proposed relative to civil pensions, including the proposition of M. Camille Crousset to abolish them entirely.

The years passed at the normal schools after the age of 20 are included in making up the years of service.

The law of 1853 provides for pensions in special cases, including those paid widows of persons who die under certain conditions in the public service.

NINETEENTH CHAPTER.
ÉCOLES MATERNELLES AND CLASSES ENFANTINES.
GENERAL ORGANIZATION.

The *écoles maternelles* are Kindergärten in which children of both sexes, from 2 to 6 years of age, receive together the care which their physical, moral and intellectual development demand.

The *classes enfantines*, annexed to a lower primary school or to an *école maternelle*, are for children of both sexes from 4 to 7 years of age. These infant classes form the mean between the *école maternelle* and the primary school. In addition to the training of the *école maternelle*, children receive primary instruction.

No child is received in an *école maternelle* without a certificate of admission, signed by the mayor, and a duly legalized medical certificate, establishing the fact that he has been vaccinated and has no contagious disease.

The training in the *écoles maternelles* and *classes enfantines* includes:
 a. Games, calisthenics with musical accompaniment;
 b. Manual exercises;
 c. First principles of moral education;
 d. Knowledge of common things;
 e. Language exercises;
 f. Elements of drawing, reading, writing and number.

The regulations touching the building and furnishing of the *écoles maternelles* are set forth below under a special head (page 72).

No one can be appointed a directress of an *école maternelle* who does not hold the *certificat d'aptitude pédagogique* and has not attained the age of 25 with two years' experience in public or private *écoles maternelles*.

The children of public *écoles maternelles* are divided into two sections according to age and development.

If the average attendance exceeds fifty, the directress has an assistant. The directress and assistant alternate in the two divisions.

A *femme de service* is attached to each *école maternelle*. This servant is appointed and discharged by the directress, with the consent of the mayor. She is paid by the commune.

The department council in each department issues regulations for the public *écoles maternelles*, following the plan of the decree of the minister in higher council.

In each commune where there is an *école maternelle*, there may be one or several committees of patronesses, presided over by the mayor. The members of these committees are appointed by the academy inspector, with the advice of the mayor. The duties of these committees are to watch over the sanitary regulations, the proper care of the establishment and the use of funds or gifts in favor of the children.

A physician appointed by the mayor visits once a week the *écoles maternelles*, entering his observations on a register kept for the purpose.

After an absence due to sickness, no child is readmitted without a medical certificate of complete recovery.

The directress reports annually in detail all matters relating to the establishment. This report is submitted to the department inspectress, or the primary inspector.

Without special permission of the primary inspector, children may not pass from the *école maternelle* or *classe enfantine* to the primary school, except in October, in January and at Easter. No *école maternelle* may receive more than 150 pupils without a special authorization from the academy inspector.

Écoles maternelles are open from March 1 to November 1, from 7 A. M. to 7 P. M., from November 1 to March 1 from 8 A. M. to 6 P. M. These hours may be modified according to local needs by the academy inspector on demand of the mayor.

Écoles maternelles may not be closed except Sundays; January 1st and 2d, Ascension day; Monday of Whitsuntide; the day of the Assumption; All Saints' day; Christmas day; the day of the national *fête*; from Thursday before Easter to Thursday after Easter; the first fortnight in August.

Directresses of *écoles maternelles*, with a single class, may not take other vacations. In *écoles maternelles*, with several classes, a vacation of one month is accorded annually to the directress or assistant alternately.

Parents neglecting to call for their children according to the rules are warned, and, if the neglect occurs again, the children are sent home to stay. This may not be done, however, except by the academy inspector on proposal of the directress and with consent of the committee of patronage. Children may take the midday meal at the school.

The *école maternelle* is to be kept in a constant state of cleanliness and salubrity. It is to be swept and scrubbed every day. The air is to be frequently renewed.

On arrival of the children at the school, the directress is to assure herself of their state of health and cleanliness. She is to exact that each be provided with a handkerchief, and that the lunch basket contain, in addition to the food, a cover and a napkin.

It is an interesting sight to see all these little ones drawn up in line undergoing the tour of inspection. Every child with dirty face or hands is whisked off at once to be scrubbed. Some of the bath-rooms are beautifully finished and furnished. They look as if they might have been made for the court of the King of Lilliput.

Before entering the exercise-hall the children are conducted to privies, where they are always watched by the directress and assistant.

Good marks, pictures and playthings are given as rewards.

At the end of each month the cards for good marks are exchanged for pictures and playthings. The distribution of prizes is not allowed.

The only punishments permitted are deprivation for a short time of the tasks and common games; recall of the cards for good marks.

Directresses and assistants may not receive presents from the pupils or parents.

Petitions, subscriptions and lotteries are not allowed.

No species of domestic animals are allowed in the parts of schools reserved for the children.

It is forbidden to overburden the memory of children with dialogues and dramatic scenes for public celebrations.

PEDAGOGIC ORGANIZATION.

In each public *école maternelle* the gradation of the pupils is made annually, at the time of the opening of the primary schools, by the directress under the control of the department inspectress, or the primary inspector.

The weekly time-table for each *école maternelle* is arranged by the directress, with the approval of the department inspectress, or of the primary inspector.

Object.— The object of the *école maternelle* is the commencement of physical, moral and intellectual education.

The *école maternelle* is not a school in the ordinary sense of the word. It forms the passage from the family to the school. It preserves the affection and indulgent gentleness of the family, and at the same time initiates into the work and regularity of the school

The success of the directress is not determined by the knowledge communicated, by the mean of instruction, by the number and duration of the tasks; but by the *ensemble* of good influences to which the child is subjected, by the pleasure he learns to take in school, by the habits of order, cleanliness, politeness,* attention, obedience and mental activity which he acquires in playing.

Directresses should not endeavor to send to the primary school children already far advanced in their instruction. They should aim to send children prepared to receive instruction. All the exercises should follow this general principle. They should aid the development of the various faculties of the child without fatigue, without constraint, without excessive application. They are intended to make him love school and to give him in early life a taste for work, never imposing tasks incompatible with the feebleness and mobility of early childhood. The end to attain, in taking into account the different temperaments, the precocity of some and the dullness of others, is not that all should attain the same knowledge of reading, writing and number; but that they know well the little they know; that they love their tasks, their games, their lessons; that they acquire no distaste for their first school exercises which become so repugnant if the patience, vivacity and ingenious affection of the mistress find no means to vary them.

Good health: hearing, sight and touch, already exercised by a graduated succession of those little games and little experiences which aid in educating the senses; childish ideas, but plain and clear, touching the first elements of that which is to be later primary instruction; a foundation of habits and dispositions on which the school may lean later in giving regular instruction; taste for gymnastics, singing, drawing, pictures, recitals; eagerness in listening, in seeing, in observing, in imitating, in questioning, in answering; a certain faculty of attention, cherished by obedience, confidence and good humor; the intelligence awakened and the soul opened to all good moral impres-

---

* Both in France and Germany teachers pay careful attention to the manners of the pupils. They are invariably polite. In France, upon the entrance of a stranger, the boys rise at once and give him the military salute, the girls rise and bow. They always remain standing until asked to take their seats. In the Kindergärten (*écoles maternelles*) politeness often takes a still more exaggerated form of salute. The pupils await standing the signal of the teacher and then throw kisses toward the stranger. This is somewhat embarrassing, as the teacher is apt to watch the guest in order to see if all these kisses are wafted back as gracefully as they are sent.

But the politeness of these school children is not confined to the class-room. After having visited many schools in Germany and France, I used to meet quite often some of the boys upon the street. They invariably removed their hats. Not once in the course of my visitations in either country did I note a case of rudeness or vulgarity.

I am compelled to admit that the lessons in manners are much more effective in French and German schools than in our own.

sions: these ought to be the effects and results of the years at the *école maternelle*. If the child has this preparation for the primary school, a few pages more or less of the primary syllabus are of little importance.

Method.—The method is indicated by the name of the establishment. It consists in imitating as closely as possible the form of training adopted by an intelligent and devoted mother.

The *école maternelle* should not develop one order of faculties at the expense of the others. All should be developed in harmony. Special methods founded on exclusive and artificial systems are not advisable. The simplest exercises of all methods should be chosen in order to form a course which will minister to the different needs of the little child and bring all his faculties into play. The exercises should have a great variety. Object lessons, conversation, singing, the first attempts at drawing, reading, number and recitation should divide the time with physical exercises, games and gymnastics. This method is essentially natural, familiar, always open to progress, and always susceptible of development and reformation.

Division of the course.—The games are divided into those for the *préau* and those for the *cour*. Separate playthings are furnished for each.

Musical instruction comprises songs in unison and in two parts which accompany the games and evolutions. The mistress uses a tuning-fork.

The manual exercises consist in plaiting, weaving, folding, stitching, cutting, knitting, bead-stringing, and the performance of tasks with cardboard, straws, sand, etc. Needlework and all other tasks of a nature to fatigue the children are forbidden.

The first principles of moral training are given in the form of familiar conversation, recitals and songs destined to inspire a sense of duty toward the family, France and God. This instruction must not be of a confessional character.

The common information (*connaissances usuelles*) includes elementary notions of clothing, food and dwelling; of man, animals, plants and rocks, of color and form, the division of time, the seasons; of the cardinal points, of France and the principal countries of the earth. This instruction is given with the aid of objects, and representations of objects.

Language work, connected with all exercises, aims to accustom the children to express their ideas simply and correctly, and to increase their vocabularies according to the development of their intelligence and of their needs.

The elements of drawing comprise,—

a. Combinations of lines by use of sticks, etc.; reproduction of these combinations on the slate, and of easy drawings of the mistress on the blackboard.

b. Reproduction on slate and paper of common objects, and of very simple ornaments.

Instruction in reading embraces only usual words and simple phrases. Children should use movable letters in learning to read.

Instruction in both reading and writing is given only to the children of the first section.

The elements of number include,—

a. The formation and representation of the numbers from one to ten, and from ten to 100 by the aid of sticks, pebbles, coin, common measures, etc., placed in the hands of pupils.

b. The four operations applied to the first hundred always with the aid of objects.

c. The representation of the first hundred by figures.

Children are exercised in mental calculation on all the numbers studied.

The recitals or stories, based as much as possible on objects or representations of objects, should embrace scenes in child-life. Anecdotes, descriptions, biographic sketches and accounts of travel should give an idea of and encourage a love for France. The intellectual exercises and the manual should alternate, and should be separated by songs and games.

The following special program illustrates the monthly division of object lessons in the first section. For full course, see pages 98–109, under Infant course.

OCTOBER.

OBJECT LESSONS.
Recitals, conversations, questions, showing the objects to the children as much as possible.
Vintage.—Vine, grape, wine.—Vat, cask, bottle, glass, stopper, liter.—Apple, cider.—Hops, beer.

DRAWING.
Drawings made by mistress on blackboard.—Pupils reproduce only those which are simple enough to find a place in the course below.
Grape, leaf, wine-press, vat, cask, bottle, glass, funnel, liter.

SONGS AND GAMES.
(To be executed by the children.) Autumn (Delbruck).—The Cooper.

NOVEMBER.

OBJECT LESSONS.
Ploughing.—Plough.—Sowing.
Lighting—Candle, wax-candle, lamp, gas.—Light-house.

DRAWING.
Plough-share, harrow.
Candle-stick, lamp, gas-burner, light-house.

SONGS AND GAMES.
Labor.—Sowing (Mme. Pape-Carpantier).

DECEMBER.

OBJECT LESSONS.

Heating.—Cold, snow, ice, avalanches; Switzerland, Alps; skates, sleighs.—Thermometers.—Stove, chimneys.—Wood, coal, matches.—Chilblains, colds.—Fireside, family.

DRAWING.

Skate, sleigh, thermometer, stove, chimney, bellows, shovel, tongs, fire-pump.

SONGS AND GAMES.

Little Chimney-sweeper (Mme. Pape-Carpantier).—Fire (Delbruck).

JANUARY.

OBJECT LESSONS.

New Year.—Movement of the earth around the sun; congratulations; New Year gifts, charity; oranges, chestnuts.

Clothing.—Furs, rugs, quilts, woolen, cotton, sheets, flannel, weaving, spinning, dyeing, needles, pins.

DRAWING.

Sphere; oranges, chestnuts; money-box. scissors, tape-line.

SONGS AND GAMES.

Winter.—Happy New Year (Delbruck).
Little Knitters (Delcasso).

FEBRUARY.

OBJECT LESSONS.

Human body.—Principal organs of the senses.

Food.—Meats and drinks; baker, butcher, fruiterer, grocer; hunger, appetite, indigestion.

DRAWING.

Eye, ear, nose, hand; kitchen range, saucepan, stove, kettle, pot, gridiron.

SONGS AND GAMES.

Gymnastics (Lainé).
Bread (Delbruck).

MARCH.

OBJECT LESSONS.

Dwelling.—Wood, stone, iron, brick; slate, plaster, lime, tile, thatch, zinc; different industries.

Bees.—Hive, cells, wax, honey.

DRAWING.

House, window, door; table, bed; chair, wardrobe, bureau, wall, layers of stone, of brick; plan of a house, frame-work; hammer, saw, pincers, square, compass, plumb-line, hod, trowel.

SONGS AND GAMES.

Little Workmen.
Bees' Patrol (Mme. Pape-Carpantier).

APRIL.

OBJECT LESSONS.

Vegetation.—Grains, roots, stems, flowers, etc.

Insects.—May beetle, caterpillar, silkworm.

Birds' nests.—Services the birds render us; swallows.

DRAWING.

Flowers, leaves, beans, peas, potatoes.

SONGS AND GAMES.

Spring (Delbruck).
Silkworm (Mme. Pape-Carpantier).

MAY.

OBJECT LESSONS.

Water.—Brook, stream, river, sea, cold baths, swimming.

Fishing.—Salt and fresh water fish.

Washing.—Soap, cleanliness.

DRAWING.

Bath-tub.
Boat, fish-hook, net, line, fish.
Bucket, pump, fountain, well, washing-beater.

SONGS AND GAMES.

Vive l'eau! (Delbruck). Bourgeois of Provence.

JUNE.

OBJECT LESSONS.
Farm.— Haymaking.— Horse, ass, shepherd-dog, wolf, sheep, pigs, turkeys, hens, geese, ducks, pigeons.— Dairy, milk, butter, cheese.

DRAWING.
Pan, churn, milk-can.

SONGS AND GAMES.
Little Shepherd.
Haymaking (Delcasso).

JULY.

OBJECT LESSONS.
Storm.— Lightning, thunder, hail, wind, lightning-rod, rainbow.
Fruits.— Cherries, strawberries, apricots, pears, apples, plums.

DRAWING.
House, lightning-rod; rainbow, umbrella.
Cherry, apricot, pear, apple, plum.

SONGS AND GAMES.
Summer.
Fruit-merchant (Delbruck).

AUGUST.

OBJECT LESSONS.
Harvest.— Wheat, barley, oats, flour, bread, dough, oven, baker, pastry-cook.
Voyages.— Highroads, railways, steamboats; map, cardinal points, compass, magnet; races of men, France, the world.

DRAWING.
Sheaf, spike of wheat; scythe, sickle; windmill, grindstone; scales, weights.
Locomotive, rails; sailboat, steamboat; oars, rudder, compass.

SONGS AND GAMES.
Game of Wheat (Mme. Pape-Carpantier).
Around the World.

SEPTEMBER.

OBJECT LESSONS.
Hunting.— Roebuck, deer, wild boar, wolf, fox, hare, rabbit, partridge, lark, quail; gun.
Village fête.— Fair, shop, fire-works, powder, money.

DRAWING.
Hunting-horn, game-bag, gun.
Coin and bank-notes.

SONGS AND GAMES.
Fox (Delcasso).

CONSTRUCTION AND FURNITURE OF ÉCOLES MATERNELLES.

The *école maternelle* comprises,

a. A vestibule with waiting-room for parents;
b. One or two exercise halls;
c. A covered and closed court (*préau*);
d. A kitchen for preparing or warming the food of the children;
e. A playground with small garden;
f. An *abri* with privies and urinals for the children;
g. Lodgings for the directress and for one or several assistants, according to necessity.

General conditions.

Art. 1.— The site should be central and airy, properly drained, accessible, removed from every noisy, insalubrious or dangerous establishment, and at least 100 meters from cemeteries.

The site must contain 400 meters, and should be reckoned at about 8 meters per child.

Art. 2.— The disposition of the buildings should be determined according to the climate, considering sanitary conditions, exposure, configuration and dimensions of site, and especially the distance of adjacent buildings.

In case the *école maternelle* form part of a *groupe scolaire*, it should not be placed between the boys' and girls' schools.

Art. 3.—All rooms used by children should be on the ground floor, which should be raised above the level of the ground by three 15 centimeter steps.

Art. 4.— No foreign service may be lodged in the school buildings.

Exercise halls.

Art. 5.— If there are several halls of exercise, they are not to be adjoining. They should communicate with the covered court (*préau*), either directly or by halls at least 1.50 meters broad.

Art. 6.— Exercise halls are to be rectangular, with 4 meter ceiling and a maximum width of 8 meters. They should be calculated to assure each child a minimum of 80 centimeters.

Art. 7.— Floor is to be of hard wood, laid as far as possible on bitumen. Pine may be used where the wood is common on condition that the strips are narrow and properly oiled. If there is no cellar, the flooring is to be laid on a platform of waterproof materials.

Art. 8.—The ceiling is to be flat and smooth. A line is to be traced thereon indicating north and south. There is to be no cornice around the walls. The angles formed by walls or partitions with each other or with the ceilings are to be rounded 10 centimeters in radius. All inside walls are to be covered with a polished coating permitting frequent cleansing. They should be wainscotted in wood to the height of 1 meter.

Art. 9.— Single doors are preferable. They should be 90 centimeters broad. Doors opening directly from the exercise halls into streets, highways or courts are not allowed.

Art. 10.— Light from the ceiling is not allowed.

The windows should be on the two longitudinal walls of the exercise halls. They should be rectangular or slightly arched. The number and dimensions should be calculated to light all parts of the hall. The distance between the bottom of the lintel and the bottom of the ceiling should be about 20 centimeters. The sill, with sloping faces, should not be more than 1.20 meters from the ground. The French sashes are to be divided horizontally into two pieces, opening separately for ventilation.

Art. 11.— Each hall is to have a stove provided with a water-box with evaporating surface. The stoves are to be covered with a double covering of metal or terra cotta. They are to be surrounded with an iron grating and are not to have either oven or dish-warmer. The stove-pipe should in no case pass over the heads of the children. The children are not to be placed nearer the stove than 1.25 meters. Cast-iron stoves *à feu direct* are forbidden.

Art. 12.— In connection with the heating, proper ventilation is to be secured. Orifices for pure air, which ought to be taken directly from the outer air, and orifices for the escape of vitiated air should have a sufficient section to prevent obstructions.

Court, kitchen and play-ground.

Art. 13.— The surface of the court is to allow about 80 centimeters for each pupil. The ceiling is to be 4 meters high.

The court is to be constructed in accordance with articles 5, 6, 7, 8, 9, 10, 11 and 12.

Art. 14.— The kitchen is to be in convenient communication with the court. It is to have air and light directly from the outer air.

The floor is to be paved with brick, tile or flagstones, or cemented.

Art. 15.— The surface of the playground should allow about three meters for each pupil. It is not to have less than 150 meters.

Art. 16.— The ground is to be covered with sand. Bitumen, pavement or cement are not to be employed except for the passages and the walks, which should never project. In case the soil slant, the declivity should never exceed three centimeters per meter. The ground is to be leveled to insure proper drainage of surface water. Slops should never cross the playground in an uncovered channel.

Art. 17.— Trees should be set out in the playground at convenient distances from the buildings, and arranged in a manner to allow necessary space for exercise and games for the children. A small garden should be annexed to the playground.

Privies.

Art. 18.— Every *école maternelle* should have separate privies for the sexes, and urinals for the boys. These should be in communication with the court (*préau*) by means of an *abri*.

Art. 19.— The privies should be so placed that prevalent winds blow not toward the buildings and the playground. They are to be divided into cabins, one for about 15 pupils. Each cabin is to be 55 centimeters in length and 80 centimeters in depth.

Art. 20.— The seat is to be of wood about 23 centimeters high and slightly inclined in front. The orifice should be oblong, about 20 centimeters by 14 centimeters. It should not be more than 5 centimeters from the edge. The basin should be furnished with a stop-valve.

Art. 21.— The urinals should be equal in number to the privies. The boxes should be about 35 centimeters wide, 25 centimeters deep and 70 centimeters high.

Art. 22.— The sides and floor of the privies and urinals should be of impervious materials. All the angles should be rounded. The privies are to be so constructed that water will run towards the seat and escape through an opening above the stop-valve. A service of water is to be provided for cleansing purposes.

Art. 23.— The vaults are to be fixed or movable. Movable vaults are preferable. They are to be provided with ventilators. Stationary vaults are to be small, but not less than 2 meters in length, breadth and height. They are to be arched, constructed of impervious materials and coated with cement. They should be stanch and the bottom should be in the form of a basin. The exterior angles should be rounded 25 centimeters in radius. They are to be placed far from the wells. They are to be fitted with a ventilating pipe, to be raised as high above the privies as the neighboring buildings make necessary.

Art. 24.— The urinals and privies are not to have bolts or other fastenings. They are to be masked by a partition 60 centimeters distant from the cabins. This partition, raised 15 centimeters from the ground, is not to be more than 70 centimeters high.

Lodgings.

Art. 25.— The lodgings of the directress are to comprise two or three rooms à feu, a kitchen, water-closet, and cellar. The floor space is to be 70 square meters.

Art. 26.— The lodgings of the assistant are to comprise one room à feu and a closet.

Art. 27.— There is to be no direct communication between the school and lodgings.

Furniture.

Art. 28.— The furniture of the exercise halls includes tables 42 centimeters high for the smaller children and 45 for the larger children. The oval form is preferable, especially for the little ones. Tables are to accommodate eight children, allowing 45 centimeters to each. Each child is to have a small chair, the seat of which is to be 22 centimeters high for the little ones and 25 for the other section.

Art. 29.— If school desks for two pupils, having stationary seats with backs, are used, the dimensions for the two sections are to be as follows:

Height above the floor 42 and 45 centimeters.
Width 40 centimeters.
Length 90 centimeters.
Height of seat 22 and 25 centimeters.
Distance between seat and desk 5 centimeters. The top of desk is to be horizontal unless made to incline, by some simple and inexpensive contrivance, for some of the exercises of the larger children.

"The back of the seat is formed by a cross-piece 8 centimeters wide, the height of which above the seat is to be 18 and 19 centimeters.

The seat is to be 20 centimeters wide.

Art. 30.— The tables or desks are not to interfere with the easy execution of the gymnastic exercises. The aisles next the wall are to be at least 80 centimeters wide.

Art. 31.— A table with drawers is to serve as teacher's desk.

Art. 32.— Blackboards are to be placed along the walls of the hall 50 centimeters from the floor, and rising 1.20 meters above the same.

Art. 33.— A cupboard is to be provided for teaching supplies.

Covered court.

Art. 34.— The furniture of the court includes hooks for clothing and open-work shelves, arranged along the walls for the lunch-baskets (The height of the shelves and hooks should be such as to permit the children to reach their things); seats with backs arranged in a circle; tables and movable seats for children's repasts (The length of the tables is to be at least 60 centimeters); one bed for each group of ten children of the lower section; lavatories with towels, placed at one extremity of the court behind an open work screen 1 meter high with entrance and way out. The floor of this part of the court is to be paved with brick, tile, flagstone or bitumen. There is to be one wash-basin for each group of ten children. The height of the same above the floor is not to exceed 50 centimeters.

Art. 35.— A cupboard is to be provided for the linen, and is to contain extra clothing for the children.

Art. 36.- Wooden benches with backs are to be placed in a circle about the playground, which is also to furnish drinking water.

Supplies.

Art. 37.—These include;

a. Collection of playthings for the covered court (*e. g.* wooden or rubber animals, dolls and dresses, lead or wooden soldiers, building blocks, flooring blocks, etc.) and for the playground (*e. g.* buckets, shovels, wheelbarrows, go-carts, jumping ropes, hoops, balls, etc.);

b. Sand for exercises in geography and construction either in court or playground;

c. Collection of sticks, staves, slats, cubes, etc.;

d. Collection of pictures;

e. Apparatus necessary for the manual exercises:

f. Slates ruled on one side in squares;

g. Collection of common objects;

h. Movable letters;

i. Terrestrial globe and wall-map of France;

j. Tuning-fork;

k. Whistle.

OBSERVATION.

The *écoles maternelles* in Paris are furnished with an abundance of apparatus. The municipal government publishes a list of teaching supplies every year, from which directresses are permitted to select up to a fixed amount.

TWENTIETH CHAPTER.
LOWER PRIMARY SCHOOLS.
GENERAL AND PEDAGOGIC ORGANIZATION.

SECTION 1.— The lower primary schools (*écoles primaires élémentaires*) are for children from 6 to 13 years of age. No pupil can be admitted before the age of 6 years if there exist in the community at a convenient distance a public *école maternelle;* before the age of 7 years, if there exist a public *classe enfantine.* Birth certificate and medical certificate of vaccination and freedom from contagious diseases are required.

Every commune is obliged to furnish public teachers with suitable lodgings and with proper school buildings, school furniture and school supplies.

The ministerial decree regulating the building and furnishing of public lower primary schools is given below under a special head (page 92).

In case lodgings are not furnished teachers, an allowance is made therefor, the amount of which is determined each year by the prefect with the advice of the municipal council and of the academy inspector (page 60).

Teachers are not under any circumstances to be distracted from their professional work during school hours nor are they to occupy themselves with matters foreign to their scholastic duties.

Children are not to be disturbed during school hours.

The morning and afternoon sessions are to last three hours each, opening at 8 A. M. and 1 P. M., respectively.

These hours may be changed according to local needs by the academy inspector on the demand of the local authorities and with the consent of the primary inspector.

The department council, with the consent of the municipal council and on the proposition of the academy inspector, may authorize the establishment of half-time schools (*écoles de demi-temps*). In this case the director is to divide the pupils into two groups. One of these groups attends school from 8 to 11 A. M., the other from 1 to 4 P. M. Parents may on demand obtain permission to have their children attend both sessions.

In schools with several classes, the exercises of the elementary and middle courses are divided by a five-minute recess, occurring every hour. In the advanced course, each of the two sessions is divided by a fifteen-minute recess.

Teachers must oversee the pupils during recesses and intermissions, and all the time they remain on the premises.

In each school there is a list, with prices of all articles with which teacher may furnish pupils. This list is signed by the primary inspector.

French is the only language to be used in teaching.*

Theatrical representations, petitions, subscriptions and lotteries are forbidden.

No book or pamphlet, printed or in manuscript, may be introduced into the school without the written authorization of the academy inspector.

The class walls are to be whitened every year and kept in a constant state of cleanliness. The class-room is to be swept and scrubbed every day. The air is to be changed frequently. Even in winter, the windows are to be opened during recesses and intermissions.

Public teachers are not permitted to receive from pupils or parents presents of any description.

---

* It is interesting to note that since my report of last year, Prussia has found it necessary to modify the regulation that from April 1, 1889, German was to be used exclusively in teaching, even in districts with a large foreign population.

Drawn by a Pupil of a Public Lower Primary School in Paris.

The only punishments of which the teacher may make use are: Bad marks; reprimands; partial deprivation of recess; detention after class; temporary suspension, not to exceed three days. Notice is to be sent immediately to the parents of the child, the local authorities and the primary inspector. Suspension of longer duration may be pronounced only by the academy inspector.

Corporal punishment is prohibited absolutely.*

Teachers are forbidden to *tutoyer* (thee and thou) their pupils.

The extraordinary holidays are

A week at Eastertide;

New Year day or Monday if this fall on Sunday or Thursday;

Monday of Whitsuntide;

The morning after All Saints' day;

Days of patronal *fêtes*;

The day of the national *fête*.

Date and duration of vacations are fixed each year by the prefect in *conseil départemental*.†

Teachers may not change class days nor absent themselves without authorization of primary inspector, and without giving notice of this authorization to the local authorities.

If the absence lasts more than three days, the authorization of academy inspector is necessary.

Leave of absence for more than fifteen days may only be granted by the prefect. Under serious and unforeseen circumstances, the teacher may absent himself without other conditions than notice to the local authorities and to the primary inspector.

Lower primary instruction includes,—

Morals and civics;

Reading and writing;

The French language;

Arithmetic, including the metric system;

History and geography, especially of France;

Object lessons and elementary scientific notions;

Elements of drawing, singing and manual training;

Gymnastic and military exercises.

---

*Italy, France and Belgium have abolished corporal punishment. Prussia, however, recognizes it as a necessity and carries it to an extent which shocks us.

†In the *lycées* and *collèges* the summer vacation is from August first to October first. In primary normal schools the summer vacation is seven weeks in length. In lower primary schools the length of the school year varies slightly in the different departments. In those schools which I have visited the school year varies from forty-two to forty-five weeks except in the *écoles maternelles* which remain in session about forty-eight weeks annually.

The department council prepares regulations for the public lower primary schools of each department after the plan of the ministerial regulation decreed in higher council.

Instruction is given in three divisions, viz., elementary, middle and advanced courses. Whatever be the number of classes and pupils, these divisions are compulsory.

The course of study is divided as follows,—

Infant section.— One or two years according as children enter at 6 or 5;

Elementary course.— Two years, from 7 to 9;

Middle course.— Two years, from 9 to 11;

Advanced course.— Two years, from 11 to 13.

In schools with one teacher and one class, there is to be no division in the middle and advanced courses. There are not to be more than two divisions for pupils under 9.

In schools with two teachers, one has charge of the middle, and advanced courses, the other of the elementary course and of the infant section if there be one.

In schools with three teachers, each course forms a distinct class.

In schools with four classes, the elementary course includes two classes and each of the other courses one class.

In schools with five classes, the elementary course includes two classes, the middle course two and the advanced course one class.

In schools with six classes, each of the three courses forms two classes, provided the number of pupils in the advanced course be not small enough for combination into a single class.

In all cases in which the same course comprises two classes, one class represents the first year, the other the second year of the course. The two classes follow the same course of study, but the lessons and exercises are so graduated that in the second year pupils review and complete the studies of the first.

In schools with more than six classes, whatever be the number of teachers, no course is to require more than two years. The classes above six, not including the infant section, are to be parallel classes.

At the beginning of each year, the pupils are divided according to their attainments into the different classes of the three courses by the director under the control of the primary inspector. The *certificat d'études* admits to the advanced course.

Each pupil receives on entering school a special blank-book which is to be preserved throughout the school course. The first task of each month in each study is entered in this book, in class and without aid, in such a manner that the progress of the pupil may be followed from year to year. There is a special blank-book for each of the three courses. Below is given a specimen page of the *cahier* for the elementary course:

NAME OF INSTITUTION.... COMMUNAL SCHOOL AT........

DATE:
....
(day, month, year)

NAME OF PUPIL: ....COURSE

Date of birth
....
Entered school
....

(Title of task)...................................

The other *cahiers* differ only in having single ruled lines instead of the four, and in being somewhat larger (40, 48 and 64 pages). These *cahiers* are carefully preserved at the school until the child finish the courses. They are then plainly bound and given to him.

In case children leave one school for another, these *cahiers* are submitted to the teacher and form the basis for classification. Each task is to be corrected by the teacher with ink or colored pencil. The primary inspector at each inspection is to place his signature under the last task written in the *cahier*.

The cover of each *cahier* contains the name and date of birth of pupil, with the date of entering and of leaving the school. The inside covers offer the following recommendations to the children:

Child:

This *cahier* is given you to be the companion and witness of your studies throughout your school life.

Every month you are to fill a few pages with the tasks which are set for you. You are to do this in class without aid either from comrade or master. You are to continue in this way throughout your school days, that is to say up to the age of 13 years or until you have obtained the *certificat d'études*.

This *cahier* will show whether you merit promotion or not. It will give you the pleasure of seeing the progress you are making. All these tasks when bound together make but a very small volume. And yet they are in a measure the *résumé* of all your childhood, the history of your six or seven years of study. You will be glad to have this *souvenir* of your school when you leave it to return no more. You will preserve carefully these modest tasks which testify to yourself and to all how you have passed your childhood.

Child, do your duty in such a way that you may look at this abstract of your school life without having occasion to blush. It is not necessary for this that you be one of the first in your class. The advantage of this *cahier* lies in the fact that it does not compare you with your comrades but with yourself. It is not to show whether you are more intelligent, more clever, more learned than other pupils; but whether, month by month and year by year, you become more expert and better informed.

Child, be diligent. This *cahier* is ready to receive the best work you can do, work which will be a credit to you and at the same time a source of pleasure to your parents and teachers. Be careful with your penmanship, your dictation, your tasks in history, geography and arithmetic. If the first pages are filled to your satisfaction, you will wish to make the following better still.

Exert yourself to make progress. It is the law of school because it is the law of life. Men are subject thereto as well as children. The *cahier* will remind you of this perhaps while inviting you to examine yourself more frequently.

Child, think also of this. One does not work for one's self alone in this world, one works also for others. Little children without thinking of it are working also for their country.

Good pupils become good citizens. If you make good use of your childhood, if you profit by all the means of instruction which the Republic takes care to offer to all her children, you will be able one day to give back to your mother country what she is giving you to-day. France needs workers and men of property such as you will become, if you lay the proper foundation here. Do not lose your time; you have no right to do this. Idlers wrong themselves no doubt, but they wrong their country still more.

Do not permit yourself to be overcome in moments of feebleness and discouragement. Take courage and say under your breath: No, I will not be useless, ungrateful toward my family, ungrateful toward France—I will work, I will do my best, not only because it is to my interest, but because it is my duty.

All competitions between public schools, in which at least all the pupils of one of the three courses do not participate, are forbidden.

Instruction given in the public primary schools has a three-fold character,— physical, moral and intellectual.

At the opening of each school year, the time-table by day and hour is prepared by the director, and after approval of primary inspector, is exposed in the class-rooms.

The division of exercises must satisfy the following general conditions,—

a. Each session is to be divided into several different exercises, separated by the reglementary recreations;

b. Exercises demanding the greatest attention, such as arithmetic, grammar and composition, should take place in the morning, or in half-time schools, at the commencement of the sessions;

c. Every lesson and every task is to be accompanied with explanations and questions;

d. Correction of tasks and recitation of lessons are to take place during the hours to which these tasks and recitations belong. Usually the tasks are corrected on the blackboard at the same time the *cahiers* are inspected. Compositions are corrected by the master outside the class.

e. The thirty hours per week (not including the time pupils may study at home or the study hours, in the preparation of tasks and lessons) should be divided as follows:

1. There is to be a daily lesson in morals in each of the first two courses in the form of a familiar talk or by means of an appropriate selection. In the advanced course, these lessons should develop methodically the course of study in *morale;*

2. Instruction in French (reading, selections explained, lessons in grammar, exercises in orthography, dictation, analysis, composition, recitation, etc.), are to occupy about two hours a day;

3. Scientific instruction is to occupy from one hour to one and one-half hours daily. Three-quarters of an hour or one hour should be devoted to arithmetic and to mathematic exercises.

The rest of the time should be devoted to object lessons and to elementary scientific notions;

4. Instruction in history and geography, including civics, should occupy about an hour daily;

5. The time devoted to penmanship should be at least one hour daily in the elementary course, and should give place gradually in the higher courses to exercises in dictation and composition;

6. Instruction in drawing begins with very short lessons in the elementary course, and occupies two or three periods weekly in the other courses;

7. Singing lessons occupy from one to two hours per week, independent of the exercises in singing which take place daily on entering and leaving the classes;

8. Gymnastics, in addition to the evolutions and exercises which may accompany the movements of the classes, occupy daily, or at least every other day, a period in the afternoon.

In communes where there are school battalions the exercises may not take place except Thursdays and Sundays. The time to be devoted thereto is determined by the military instructor in concert with the school inspector.

9. Finally, for both boys and girls, two or three hours weekly are to be devoted to manual training.

SECTION 2.—In each department a list is made annually of the books which may be used in public primary schools. As in Prussia, text-books are not printed by the government.*

The teachers (*titulaires*) of each canton, united in special conference, make by the fifteenth of July at the latest a list of the books which they deem proper for use in public primary schools.

All these lists are sent to the academy inspector. A commission sitting at the chief place in the department, and composed of the primary inspector, the director and the directress of the normal schools and delegated professors and masters of these establishments, meets under the presidency of the academy inspector, revises the cantonal lists, and issues the catalogue for the department which is then submitted to the rector for his approval.

---

* American text-books are recognized by impartial persons as the best in the world, both as regards mechanical construction and subject matter. This superiority is attributed to the independence and spontaneity of the authors. Manuel Valdés Rodriguez in his "Problema de la Educacion," published at Havana in 1891 says: "Bien puede decirse que apénas habrá en el mundo libros mejor constituidos por sus condiciones, así internas, como externas. Comparados con los franceses los (los libros de texto americano) son muy superiores en uno y otro concepto. Débese esta superioridad á las condiciones de independencia y espontaneidad de los autores."

The records which the male and female teachers must keep are,—
a. Register of matriculation;
b. Register of absence and attendance;
c. Inventory of school furniture and school supplies;
d. Inventory of personal property, if there be any;
e. Catalogue of the books of the popular library of the public school, with record of receipts and disbursements and books drawn.

The first four of these records must be kept also by the directresses of the *écoles maternelles*.

In addition to the records referred to above, there is a very convenient little book, entitled *carnet de correspondance*, which contains a record of absences, tardy marks, deportment, work at school, work at home and relative standing of pupils. This book is given to the pupil every fortnight on Saturday, and is returned Monday morning with the remarks of parents or guardians written over their signatures.

Below is printed a specimen page of this book of record:

.... *Class.*   .... *Course.*

SEPTEMBER, 189..
Second Fortnight.

Absence ....
Tardiness ....
Deportment at school ....
School work ....
Home tasks ....
Relative standing { ....
                   ....
General note for the fortnight ....

REMARKS.

Teacher.	Parents.
Visa of teacher.	Signature of parents.

In France great stress is laid on encouraging the habit of saving money. The inside cover of this little *carnet de correspondance* contains an account of the savings of the children for the year in the following form:

No........   GRAND SAVINGS BANK,
                                              No. of Bank-book........

SCHOOL SAVINGS BANK.

M..

born.......................... 18..., at ....

residing at ....

MONTH (School year 189..-189..).	Weekly Deposits.					Total for month.	To grand savings bank.
	1	2	3	4	5		
September...............							
October							
November...............							
December							
January (189).........							
February							
March							
April							
May							
June							
July......................							
August							

Total deposits for year........
Amount transferred...........
Balance ....

Totals ....

The child deposits his savings with teacher weekly, penny by penny. When the amount thus deposited equals a *franc* it is entered by the teacher on the Savings Bank-book, which is exactly like those used by adults.

Those who have not given this subject attention would be surprised to learn the grand total of such savings (page 31). But pennies generally contributed make up very large sums. In England, for example, the children's pence have been an important source of income.

The last education report, reviewed July 22, 1891, in the London Globe, shows that the children's pence for the year under review exceeded £1,900,000.

This is most remarkable seeing that over a million of children who ought to have attended the English public elementary schools were not found there.*

DIVISION OF THE COURSE OF STUDY IN LOWER PRIMARY SCHOOLS.

I.

PHYSICAL EDUCATION.

Object.— Physical education serves a double purpose:

It fortifies the body and strengthens the constitution of the child, placing him in hygienic conditions most favorable for his general physical development.

It gives him early in life that address and agility, that manual dexterity of movement especially necessary to the pupils of primary schools, most of whom are destined for the trades. Without losing its essential character as an educational establishment, and without transformation into a work-shop, the primary school can give and ought to give physical training, which will predispose and prepare in a certain measure the boys for the duties of workmen and soldiers, the girls for household duties and the work of women.

Method.— Physical exercises form a diversion from school duties and lessons proper. It is an easy matter to conduct them in such a way that the pupils will regard them as a veritable recreation. The progress of instruction in gymnastics is regulated in detail by manuals published under the auspices of the minister, as well as by the directions of special professors and teachers. For the manual training of the boys, the exercises are divided into two groups.

One includes those which are destined to make the fingers flexible and to promote dexterity, rapidity, and accuracy of move-

---

* This is merely an illustration. The savings of French children belong to them The pence which the English children handed their teachers every Monday morning went toward defraying the cost of education. The new bill, which went into effect September 1, 1891, makes education free, thus doing away with the children's pence.

ment; the other includes graduated exercises in modeling which complement the study of drawing, and particularly of industrial drawing.

The manual training of girls, in addition to needlework and cutting, includes certain lessons, counsels and exercises by means of which the mistress does not propose to give a complete course in domestic economy, but may inspire girls, by a number of practical examples, with the love of order, leading them to acquire the serious qualities of the housekeeper, and putting them on their guard against frivolous or dangerous tastes.

II.

Intellectual Education.

Object.— The intellectual education, which the public primary schools should give, is easy to characterize.

The information imparted should be limited, but of such a character as to assure for the child the practical knowledge which he will need in life. It should act on his faculties, form and cultivate his mind and constitute in fact an education.

The ideal of the primary school is not to teach much, but to teach well.

The child learns little, but knows that little well. The instruction which he has received is limited, but not superficial. It is not a demi-instruction, and he who receives it will not be a demi-savant. That which makes instruction complete or incomplete is not the extent of the domain which is cultivated; it is the manner of cultivation.

"The object of primary instruction," wrote Gréard in 1875, "is not to embrace under the different subjects on which it touches all that it is possible to know, but to learn well under each where ignorance is inexcusable."

Method.— The object of primary instruction being thus defined, the method to follow suggests itself. It does not consist of a succession of mechanic processes or of an apprenticeship only in reading, writing and arithmetic, or of a cold series of lessons setting forth the different chapters of a course.

The only proper method in primary instruction is that which keeps up a continual interchange of ideas under varied, elastic and ingeniously graduated forms. The master begins always with what the pupils know, and proceeding from the known to the unknown, from the easy to the difficult, conducts them by a chain of oral

Lelu

Application. Nelleté
Sobriété

Le 1 Mai
1888

Français.

Ignorance et cruauté (Suite)

Il n'est pas d'un homme mais d'une brute de prendre plaisir à torturer un animal. L'animal serait nuisible debarassons nous en par la mort mais gardons nous de faire souffrir dans le but seul de faire souffrir. Ce serait dessecher en nous un des plus nobles sentiments de compassion.

Qui se complait à torturer les bêtes ne peut compatir aux misères de ses semblables. C'est un cœur dur enclin au mal qui s'il n'y prend garde eveil entretient de feroces instinct lesquels les meneront peut être quelque jour aux immenses conséquences du crime.

Deuxième partie.

Faire une observation grammaticale sur les mots soulignés une fois

Tort	Nom commun féminin singulier complément direct de débarrasser.
Ce	Pronom Démonstratif masculin singulier complément direct de dessécher.
Le	Pronom personnel mis pour homme masculin singulier.
Sera	Verbe être futur simple 3e personne du singulier.

Troisième partie.

Relevez les mots soulignés deux fois et mettre dans une colonne les principaux dérivés avec une initiale indiquant la partie du discours à laquelle il appartient.

Brute (adj.)	Brutal adj.	Brutalement (adv.)	Brutaliser (à act.)	Brutalité (n f.)
Griffer (v a.)	Griffant (adj.)	Griffure (n c.)	Griffeleux (adj.)	
Dessécher (v a.)	Desséché (adj.)	Dessèchement (n c.)	Desséchant (adj.)	

Language Exercise by French Elementary Pupil of the Middle Course.
Introduced to show that moral instruction is often given incidentally in connection with other subjects. The selection sets forth the evils of ignorance and cruelty.

questions or of written tasks to discover the consequences of a principle, the applications of a rule, or inversely the principles and rules which they have already unconsciously applied. In all instruction the master begins with the concrete; then little by little pupils are exercised in developing the idea of the abstract, in comparing, in generalizing, in reasoning without the aid of material examples.

Primary instruction is sustained by an incessant appeal to the attention, to the judgment, to the intellectual spontaneity of the pupil. It is essentially intuitive and practical: Intuitive, that is to say it counts before all on good common sense, on the weight of evidence, on that innate power of the mind to seize, at first sight and without demonstration, not all truths, but the most simple and the most fundamental; practical, that is to say it never forgets that primary pupils have no time to lose in idle discussions, in learned theories, in scholastic curiosities, and proceeds at once to furnish them with the little store of ideas which they will need in life, and in such a manner that these ideas are preserved and developed when school days are over.

It is under this double condition that primary instruction undertakes the education and the culture of the mind. Nature herself directs the course of this instruction. It develops in parallel lines the different faculties of the intelligence merely by exercising them in a simple, spontaneous and almost instinctive manner. It forms the judgment in leading the child to judge; the habit of observation in teaching him to observe; reasoning, in aiding him to reason for himself and without the rules of logic.

This confidence in natural forces, and this absence of all pretention, suit all rudimentary instruction, but are peculiarly adapted to the public primary school, which ought to deal, not with certain children apart, but with the masses of the child population.

Instruction is necessarily collective and simultaneous. The master is not to devote himself to a few but to all. His work ought to be appreciated, not by results obtained with a portion of his class but with the class as a whole. Whatever the inequality in the intelligence of the pupils, there is a minimum of information and of aptitude which primary instruction ought to communicate to all pupils with very few exceptions. This minimum will be very easily reached by some pupils, but if it is not attained by the rest of the class, the master has not understood his task or has not entirely accomplished it.

III.
Moral Education.

Object and Method.— Moral education differs profoundly in its end and in its essential character from the other two parts of the program.

End and Essential Character.

Moral instruction is destined to complete and to bind together, to raise and to ennoble all the other instruction of the school. While each of the other studies develops a special order of aptitudes and gives useful information, this tends to develop the man himself within the man, that is to say a heart, an intelligence, a conscience.

Moral instruction moves in another sphere than physical and intellectual. The force of moral training depends much less on the precision and on the logical sequence of the truths taught than on the intensity of feeling, the vivacity of impressions and the contagious heat of conviction. This education does not lead to knowledge (*savoir*) but to will (*vouloir*). It moves more than it proves; it comes rather from the heart than from the reason. It does not undertake to analyze all the reasons for the moral act; it seeks before all to produce this act, to repeat it, to make it rule life as a habit. Especially at the primary school, it is not a science but an art, the art of inclining the free-will toward the good.

Part of the Teacher in this Instruction.

The teacher is charged with this part of education, in addition to the others, as a representative of society.

A secular and democratic society has in fact the most direct interest in the early initiation of all its members by ineffaceable lessons into the sentiment of their dignity and into a feeling not less profound of their duty and of their personal responsibility.

To attain this end, the teacher is not to teach in detail theoretic and practical morals as if dealing with children devoid of all previous notions of good and bad. The great majority enter school receiving or having received a religious instruction which familiarizes them with the idea of a God, creator of the universe and father of men, with the traditions, beliefs and practices of the Christian or Jewish religions.

By means of one of these religions and under the forms peculiar thereto, pupils have already received the fundamental notions of universal and eternal morals; but these notions are new-born and

Jachmes
Gabrielle Nellele Application 1868
Le 5 Avril

Français.

Soyez réservés et modestes

Vous serez bien _étonnés_, quand vous serez sortis du collège, de voir que les tapageurs, que les violents, que les bruyants de la cour et que les héros de la récréation et de la retenue une fois entrés dans le monde s'y évanouiront comme _des_ ombres, et que ce sont les modestes au contraire les travailleurs ceux qui faisaient tranquillement leur petite affaire, qui peu à peu sortant de la foule, se distinguent, puis sont distingués, et en arrivent enfin à devenir des hommes utiles à eux mêmes, utiles à leur Patrie !

2ᵐᵉ Tâche

Rapporter les observations faites en classe sur les mots soulignés

Étonnés. Participe passé employé avec l'auxiliaire être s'accorde avec le sujet du verbe : vous masculin pluriel

Des Adjectif indéfini féminin pluriel qualifie

ombres

Peu à peu... Locution adverbiale, signifiant *insensiblement*, adverbe de manière.

3ᵉ Partie

La terminaison *ite* ajoutée à certains mots indique une maladie inflammatoire.

D'après cela, trouver cinq (mots) noms de maladies ayant cette terminaison, et mettre leur signification en regard.

Mots simples	Mots dérivés	Sens du dérivé
Bronches	Bronch*ite*	Maladie provenant de l'inflamm. des bronches
Poitrine	Poitr*ite*	Maladie provenant de l'inflamm. de la poitrine
Méninges	Mening*ite*	Maladie provenant de l'inflamm. des méninges
Larynx	Laryng*ite*	Maladie provenant de l'inflamm. du larynx
Périchondre	Périchondr*ite*	Maladie provenant de l'inflamm. Périchondre

Language Exercise by French Elementary Pupil of the Advanced Course.
Introduced to show that moral instruction is often given incidentally in connection with other subjects. The selection teaches the value of modesty, reserve and diligence.

fragile shoots. They have not penetrated deeply into the soil; they are fugitive and confused, committed to memory rather than to conscience. They need to be ripened and developed by a suitable training, which the public teacher is to give.

The limits to his mission are, therefore, closely defined. He is to strengthen, to root in the souls of his pupils for all their lives, making them matters of daily practice, those essential notions of morality, which are common to all doctrines and necessary to all civilized men. He can accomplish this without adherence or opposition to any of the religious beliefs of his pupils. He takes the children as they come with their ideas and language and family beliefs. He has no other task than to teach them to draw therefrom what is most precious from a social standpoint, that is the doctrine of a high morality.

Object Proper and Limits of this Instruction.

Secular moral instruction is distinguished therefore from religious instruction without contradicting it. The teacher is not the substitute for priest or father. He joins his efforts with theirs in making of each child an honest man. He ought to dwell on the duties which unite men, and not on the dogmas which divide them. Every theologic and philosophic discussion is forbidden him by the nature of his duties, by the age of his pupils, by the confidence of families and of the State. His is the practical task of causing all his pupils to serve the effective apprenticeship of a moral life.

Later, when they have become citizens, the pupils may be separated by dogmatic opinions; but they will be in accord in the practice of putting the aim of life as high as possible; in having the same horror of everything base and vile, the same admiration for that which is noble and generous, the same delicate sense of duty in aspiring toward moral perfection, cost what it may; in feeling themselves united in the general religion of the good, the beautiful and the true, which is also a form and not the least pure of religious fervor.

The teacher by his character, by his conduct, by his language is himself to set the most persuasive of examples. In this kind of instruction, that which does not come from the heart does not go to the heart. A master who recites precepts, who speaks of duty without conviction, without fervor, does worse than waste his time; he commits a fault. A course in morals, regular but cold, hackneyed and dry, does not teach morals, because it does not inspire love. The simplest story in which the child finds a trace of seriousness, a single sincere word, is worth more than a long succession of mechanical lessons.

On the other hand and it seems scarcely necessary to formulate this prescription — the master should shun as a bad action everything which, in his language or in his attitude, might disturb the religious beliefs of the children confided to his care; all that might trouble them; all that might betray on his part a lack of respect or reserve.

His sole obligation and it is compatible with respect for all creeds — is to watch, in a practical and paternal fashion, the moral development of his pupils, manifesting therefor the same degree of solicitude with which he follows their intellectual and physical development. He ought not to feel that he has performed his duty toward any one of his pupils, if he has not done as much for the education of the character as for that of the intelligence. Then only does the teacher merit the title *educator*, and primary instruction the name *liberal education*.

CONSTRUCTION AND FURNITURE OF LOWER PRIMARY SCHOOLS.

The lower primary school comprises:

1. A cloak room or vestibule serving as cloak-room;
2. One or more class-rooms;
3. A covered court (*préau*) with gymnasium, and often (in schools with less than three classes) a little workshop for manual training;
4. A playground and garden, when possible;
5. Water-closets and urinals;
6. Lodgings for teacher, and for assistant teachers;

In addition, when necessary, in schools of more than three classes:

7. Lodgings for the *concierge*;
8. Waiting room for parents;
9. Study for teacher;
10. Parlor for assistant teachers;
11. Class-room for drawing with a closet for models;
12. A workshop for manual training in boys' schools or a room for needlework and cutting in girls' schools;
13. A gymnasium.

GENERAL CONDITIONS.

Art. 1.— The site should be central, easy of access, properly drained, removed from every unhealthful, noisy or dangerous establishment, and at least 100 meters distant from cemeteries.

Art. 2.— The size of the site should be sufficient to allow about 10 meters for each pupil; it should never be less than 500 meters. The school and its annexes are to be inclosed.

Art. 3.— In placing the buildings, hygienic conditions are to meet due consideration.

Art. 4.— When the mayoralty is in the school building, it should be separated therefrom. No foreign service is to be installed in the school building.

Art. 5.— The walls are not to be less than 45 centimeters in thickness if of stone, or 35 centimeters if of brick.

Art. 6.— Materials which are too permeable should not be used. Tile and slate should be used for roofing in preference to metal.

Art. 7.— The ground floor should be 60 centimeters above the soil.

Art. 8.— If there is no cellar, the flooring should be laid on an impermeable bed.

Art. 9.— In every *groupe scolaire* the buildings should be independent of each other, provided with separate entrances. The *école maternelle* should not be placed between the boys' and girls' school.

Art. 10.— A *groupe scolaire* should not embrace more than 750 pupils,— 300 boys, 300 girls and 150 infants for the *école maternelle*.

Lodgings of the Concierge.

Art. 11.— When the school has a *concierge*, the lodgings should be on the ground floor, and should include: A lodge, a kitchen, one or two rooms, water-closet and cellar. The waiting-room for parents should be near the janitor's lodge.

Cloak-rooms.— Halls.— Stairways.

Art. 12.— Each class should have a cloak-room, but the same cloak-room may be used by two or more contiguous classes. The cloak-rooms should be provided with pegs for the wraps, and with shelves for the lunch-baskets. In rural schools the vestibule may serve as cloak-room.

Art. 13. — Each class should have an independent entrance. Doors should not open directly into the street or court.

Art. 14.— If classes are entered through halls, the same should be at least 1.50 meters wide, and should be aired and lighted from without.

Art. 15.— Classes above the ground floor should be reached by straight stairways. Every thirteen or sixteen steps should be separated by a landing. The steps should be 1.35 meters wide, from 28 to 30 centimeters deep, and not more than 16 centimeters high. The bars should be 13 centimeters apart, and the hand-rail should be provided with knobs not more than 1 meter apart. There should be a second hand-rail along the walls.

Art. 16.— Every school receiving 300 pupils above the ground floor is to be provided with two stairways.

CLASS.

Art. 17.— The maximum number of places per class is fifty.

Art. 18.— The class-room should be rectangular, with a floor-space of 1.25 meters for each pupil. The ceiling should in no case be less than 4 meters high.

Art. 19.— The openings should be disposed so that each desk receive the proper light. The windows should be rectangular or slightly arched. The space between the top of the windows and the ceiling should be about 20 centimeters. The window-sills should be smooth and about 1.20 meters above the floor. Where class-rooms are lighted from one side, the light must reach the pupils from the left under the following conditions:

a. The height of the class-room should be about two-thirds of its width;

b. Ventilators should be placed in the opposite walls.

In all cases the windows should never be less than 8 meters from neighboring buildings.

Art. 20.— Windows should never be placed opposite the teacher's desk or those of the pupils. Windows in the ceiling are not allowed.

Art. 21.— The French sashes should be divided into two parts horizontally for ventilating purposes.

Art. 22.— The ceilings are to be smooth. A north and south line is to be traced thereon. There is to be no cornice. The angles made by the walls are to be rounded (radius 10 centimeters). The walls are to be smooth, permitting frequent cleansing. If not wainscotted with wood, the walls are to be cemented to the height of 1.20 meters.

Art. 23.- The floors are to be of hard wood, laid, as far as possible, on bitumen. Pine may be used in localities where this wood abounds, provided the strips of flooring are narrow and well oiled.

Art. 24.— Single doors are preferable. They should be 90 centimeters wide.

Art. 25.- Class-rooms in mixed schools are not to be divided by partitions. Boys and girls are to be grouped separately.

Art. 26.— A stove should be placed in each class-room with a water reservoir with surface for evaporation. Stoves should be provided with a double metallic covering or with one of terra cotta. They are to be surrounded with a screen and are not to have ovens. Stove-pipes should never pass over the heads of children. Pupils are not to be placed within less than 1.25 meters of the stove. Stoves à feu direct are not allowed.

Art. 27—Class-rooms are to be properly ventilated.

SALLE FOR DRAWING.— WORKSHOP FOR MANUAL TRAINING.

Art. 28.—Schools with four or more classes are to be provided with a separate room for drawing. The size of this room should allow 1.50 meters for each pupil. There is to be a closet for the models.

Art. 29.— All boys' schools should be provided with a workshop for manual training. In schools with less than three classes, this workshop may be placed in the court (préau).*

In all girls' schools with more than three classes, a room is to be provided for instruction in needlework and cutting.

COVERED COURT (PREAU).— DEPENDENCIES OF THE PREAU.— GYMNASIUM.

Art. 30.— Every school is to be provided with a covered court or abri, allowing about 1.25 meters for each pupil. The ceiling is to be 4 meters high. This court is to be furnished with lavatories and tables.

Art. 31.— There is to be a cooking stove near the court to prepare or warm the pupils' food.

Art. 32.— If there is no special gymnasium, the gymnastic apparatus may be placed in the court.

PLAYGROUND.—GARDEN.

Art. 33.—The area of the playground should be sufficient to allow five square meters for each pupil. It should never be less than 200 square meters.

Art. 34.—The surface should be sanded. Bitumen, pavement or cement may not be used except for walks and passages. Slops should not cross the playground in an open channel.

Art. 35.—There should be a small garden in the playground, with trees set out at a suitable distance from the buildings. Benches are to be placed about the playground, which is to have also a pump or fountain.

In mixed schools the playground is to be divided by a screen of lattice work.

---

*About two-thirds of the boys' elementary schools in Paris now have workshops for joining, turning, wood-carving and forging. Manual training is an essential part of the course in all lower primary schools.

PRIVIES AND URINALS.—VAULTS.

Art. 36.—Boys' schools are to have two and girls' schools three cabins for each class. A cabin is to be reserved for teachers.

Art. 37.—The privies should be so situated that they may be easily supervised, and that the prevailing winds blow not toward the buildings or the playground. The cabins are to be about 70 centimeters wide and 1.10 meters deep. The doors should open outwards, and should be raised 20 centimeters above the floor. They should be 1.10 meters high. The stone, cement or metal seat should be 20 centimeters high, and should incline toward the orifice. The oblong orifice should be 20 centimeters by 14 centimeters, and about 10 centimeters from the edge.

In mixed schools there are to be separate accommodations for the sexes.

Art. 38.—Boys' schools are to have urinals equal in number to the privies at least. The dimensions of the cabins are to be about 35 by 80 by 40 centimeters. Water is to be provided for cleansing.

Art. 39.— Same as *Art.* 22, page 75.

Art. 40.—Same as *Art.* 23, page 75.

LODGINGS OF TEACHER.— LODGINGS OF ASSISTANT TEACHERS.

Art. 41.— The lodgings of the teacher include a dining-room, two or three living-rooms, a kitchen, water-closet and cellar. The total floor-space should be from 70 to 90 square meters. The teacher's study should be on the ground floor, and as near as possible to the class-rooms and parlor.

Art. 42.— There should be no direct communication between the class-rooms and the lodgings of the teacher.

Art. 43.— The lodging of assistant teachers comprise a sleeping apartment and study.

Art. 44.— One stairway may serve for several lodgings.

Art. 45.— In schools, with four or more classes, a room on the ground floor is to serve as cloak-room and refectory for the assistant teachers.

FURNITURE AND TEACHING SUPPLIES.

Art. 46.- Lower primary schools are to be furnished by the communes with:

a. For each class:

Teachers' desk and platform; desks sufficient in number for the members of the class; black-board, crayon and erasers; reading-charts for the elementary division; a metric chart or compendium;

wall-maps — the department, France, Europe, the world or the planisphere; a stove or heater, a coal-hod.

b. Simple tools of the principal trades; necessary materials for the instruction in manual training; guns and racks (for boys' schools); gymnastic apparatus; poles, rings, ladders, knotted ropes, horizontal and parallel bars, dumb-bells, horizontal beam, rods, canes, trapeze.

c. Objects necessary for use in cleansing the school, brooms, buckets, dusters, watering pots, shovels;

d. A book-case;

e. Pegs for clothing and shelves for lunch-baskets;

f. Records such as that of matriculation, the inventory of school property, the catalogue of the school library, the record of the loans, the account of receipts and expenditures.

Art. 47.—A table with drawers, placed on a platform from 30 to 32 centimeters high is to serve as teachers' desk.

Art. 48.—Pupils' desks should be single or double. The former are preferable.*

Four types are prescribed for schools in communes not having an *école maternelle:*

Type I is for children whose height is from 1 meter to 1.10 meters;
Type II is for those from 1.11 to 1.20 meters tall;
Type III is for children from 1.21 to 1.35 meters in height;
Type IV is for pupils from 1.36 to 1.50 meters tall.

Type I is not used in schools which do not receive children under six.

A fifth type may be used for pupils more than 1.50 meters tall.

The number of the type is to be indicated on each desk. Example: III, 1^m 21 à 1^m 35.

Teachers are to measure pupils annually at the opening of the term, and assign them to the proper desks.

Desks are to be provided with glass or porcelain ink-wells, placed at the right of each pupil. They are to have a receptacle for books. Bars and supports for the feet are not allowed.

Art. 49. Blackboards should be of slate.

Art. 50. This article prescribes the form and arrangement of the tables and seats used in drawing.

---

* French school furniture is better than Prussian though inferior to American. Desks or five and six pupils are still found in many country schools and in some city schools.

OFFICIAL PROGRAMS OF INSTRUCTION IN LOWER PRIMARY SCHOOLS.

ACCORDING TO THE LAW OF OCTOBER 30, 1886, AND TO THE DECREES OF JANUARY 18, 1887 (*Les Nouveaux Programmes des Ecoles primaires* — 1889).

PART I.—PHYSICAL EDUCATION.

	Infant course. From 5 to 7 years.	Elementary course. From 7 to 9 years.	Middle course. From 9 to 11 years.	Advanced course. From 11 to 13 years.
1. Health and cleanliness.	Inspection of children on arrival; supervision of their games from hygienic standpoint; particular care for the feeble.	Inspection of children on arrival and at their entry into the class; exact absolute cleanliness; supervise their games; practical advice, either in common or in particular, touching food, clothing, bearing and habits.	Continue the same course of instruction and education.	Continue the same course of instruction and education.
2. Gymnastics. (Follow the distinct manuals for boys and girls, published by the ministry.)	Games, *rondes*, evolutions, rhythmic movements, graduated exercises.	Preparatory exercises; movements of arms and legs; dumb-bell and bar exercises; running in time; evolutions.	Continue exercises in bending and stretching the arms and legs; dumb-bell exercises; exercises with the bar, rings, ladder, knotted rope, horizontal bars, parallel bars, poles, trapeze; evolutions.	Continue the same exercises; exercises in balancing on one foot; movements of the arms in walking; double exercises with the bar; running; leaping; stick exercises (for the boys).
3. Military exercises. (For the boys.)			Marching, alignment, formation of platoons, etc. Preparation for military training.	Military training. School of the soldier without arms. Principles of the different steps; alignment; marches, counter-marches and halts. Changes of direction.
4. Manual training. (For the boys.)	Exercises in plaiting, folding, weaving.	Manual exercises to develop dexterity.	Construction of objects in cardboard, covered with colored drawings and colored paper.	Exercises combined with drawing and modeling: Plans of objects and construction after the plans, or *rice versa*. Study of the principal tools employed in wood-work; practical graduated exercises; planing, sawing of woods, elm-
	Cutting and sticking pieces of colored paper on geometric drawings. Basket-work.	Cutting cardboard in the form of geometric solids.	Little tasks with wire; trellis work.	
		Basket-work; sprigs of different colors.	Combinations of wire and wood.	

99

Combinations in colored worsteds on canvass or paper.	Modeling: reproduction of geometric solids and of very simple objects.	Modeling; simple architectural ornaments.	ple joints; boxes nailed or joined without nails; wood-turning, turning of very simple objects.
		Notions of the most common tools.	Study of the principal tools employed in iron-work; exercises with files, trimming or completion of objects from forge or foundry.

5. Manual training. (For the girls.)

Little Froebel exercises: Plaiting, folding, weaving.	Knitting and study of the stitch; plain stitch, purling, widening, narrowing; marking stitch on canvass.	Knitting and crocheting. Marking canvass.	Knitting of petticoats, waistcoats, gloves.
Simple exercises in knitting.	Elements of needlework: hemming and over-handing; manual exercises to develop dexterity; cutting and application of pieces of colored paper; modest attempts at modeling.	Elements of needlework: running stitch, side stitch, back stitch, over-casting stitch, simple seam, hem, fell, over-handing on selvage, on folds. Making of simple and easy articles of needlework (towels, napkins, handkerchiefs, aprons, *chemises*), patchwork.	Marking linen. Quilting, gathering, buttonholes, mending garments, darning. Notions of cutting and making of the easiest garments. Simple ideas of domestic economy, and application to cookery, to the washing and care of linen, to the *toilette*, to the care of house, garden and farmyard. Practical exercises at school and at home.

PART II.—INTELLECTUAL EDUCATION.

	Infant course — 5 to 7.	Elementary course — 7 to 9.	Middle course — 9 to 11.	Advanced course — 11 to 13.
1. Reading	First exercises in reading. Letters, syllables, words.	Connected reading with explanation of words.	Connected reading with explanations.	Expressive reading.
2. Writing	First elements	Coarse, medium and fine writing.	Ordinary cursive writing	Cursive, round-hand, *bâtarde*.
3. French language	Exercises in language, reading and writing preparatory to orthography.	First notions, given orally, of the noun (the number and gender), the adjective, the pronoun, the verb (first elements of conjugation). Idea of the formation of the plural and of the feminine; of agreement of adjective with noun, of verb with subject. Idea of a simple proposition.	Elementary grammar: the ten parts of speech; conjugations; notions of syntax; general rules for the past participle; notions on word families, derivatives and compounds; principles of punctuation.	Review of grammar and syntax. Study of the proposition and of the different kinds of propositions. Functions of words in the phrase. Principal rules for the use of words and for the sequence of tenses. Difficulties in orthography in certain nouns, pronouns, adjectives and irregular verbs. Notions of etymology and of derivation.
	a. Oral exercises.— Familiar questions with the object of teaching correct expression, and correction of local faults in pronunciation and accent.	*a*. Oral exercises.—Questions and explanations, especially in the course of the reading lesson or in the correction of tasks. Questions on the meaning, use and orthography of the words of the text read; spelling of difficult words.	*a*. Oral exercises.—Elocution and pronunciation; grammatic questions; oral reproduction of stories, *résumés* of pieces read in class.	*a*. Oral exercises.—Continuation and development of the elocutionary exercises. Oral accounts of stories, of lessons, of walks, of experiences, etc.
		Oral reproduction of short phrases read and explained, then of stories or of fragments of stories told by the teacher.		Oral *exposé* of an historic or literary selection, which the pupil has been told to read or analyze.

b. Memory exercises.—Recitation of simple poems. c. Written exercises.—Dictation of a word, then of two or three words, then of very simple phrases.	Brief selections read by the mistress are listened to and reproduced by the pupils.	b. Memory exercises.—Recitation of simple poems. c. Written exercises.—Graduated dictation exercises in orthography; short grammatical exercises of various forms; written reproductions (on blackboard, on slate, on *cahier*) of phrases previously explained; composition of short phrases with given elements. d. Exercises in analysis.—Grammatical analysis (generally oral, sometimes written). Analysis of the proposition into its essential parts. e. The master reads aloud twice a week a selection interesting to children of the class.	b. Memory exercises.—Recitation of fables, of short poems, of prose selections. c. Written exercises.—Dictation taken as much as possible from the classics and without examination of grammatical difficulties: exercises in invention, in construction of phrases, homonyms, synonyms; mutual correction by the pupils of dictation and other exercises; free written reproduction of selections read in class or at home, and of stories told by the teacher; exercises in composition on simple subjects familiar to children. d. Exercises in analysis.—Grammatical analysis, generally oral. Logical analysis, limited to fundamental distinctions. e. The master reads aloud twice a week selections from the classics.	b. Memory exercises.—Expressive recitation of choice selections in prose and poetry, in dialogues, in scenes from the classics. c. Written exercises.—Dictation from the classics without examination of grammatical difficulties, exercises on the derivation and composition of words, on etymology, on the application of the most important rules of syntax. Compositions on simple subjects.—Written accounts of lessons and selections read. d. Exercises in analysis.—Questions in grammatical analysis relating to difficulties encountered in selections read; oral exercises in logical analysis. e. Master and pupils read together selections on literary, dramatic and historic subjects.
4. History	Anecdotes, biographies drawn from natural history, stories, accounts of travel. Explanation of pictures.	Accounts and familiar talks on the greatest personages and principal facts of national history up to the 100 years' war.	Elementary course in the history of France, dwelling emphatically on the essential facts since the 100 years' war. *Example of trimonthly division.* a. 1328 to 1610. b. 1610 to 1789. c. 1789 to the present. d. Review.	Methodic review of French history: deeper study of the modern period: summary notions of general history; for antiquity, Egypt, the Jews, Greece, Rome; for the middle ages and modern times, great events especially as bearing on French history.

PART II.—INTELLECTUAL EDUCATION—(Continued).

	Infant course—5 to 7.	Elementary course—7 to 9.	Middle course—9 to 11.	Advanced course—11 to 13.
5. Geography	Familiar conversations and simple preparatory exercises, cultivating the habit of observation by causing the children to note common phenomena.	Continuation and development of the exercises of the infant class. The cardinal points not learned by heart, but found on the spot, in the court, in the walks, by the sun's position. Observation exercises.—The seasons, common atmospheric phenomena, the horizon, the sun, etc. Explanation of geographic terms (mountains, rivers, seas, gulfs, isthmuses, straits, etc.), starting with objects seen by the pupils, and proceeding by analogy. Preparation for the study of geography by the intuitive and descriptive method. *a.* Local geography (house, street, hamlet, *commune, canton,* etc.). *b.* General geography (the earth, its form and size, grand divisions and subdivisions). Ideas of maps, reading; chart and map elements of chart and map reading; terrestrial globe, continents and oceans; talks on the native place.	Geography of France and her colonies; physical geography; political geography, with detailed study of the *canton,* of the department, of the region. Exercises in map-drawing on the blackboard and in the *cahier,* without tracing.	Review and development of the geography of France; physical and political geography of Europe; general geography of other parts of the world. The French colonies. Map-drawing from memory.
6. Civics		Informal explanations, in connection with reading, of words suggesting national ideas; citizen, soldier, army, native country; commune, department, nation; law, justice, public force.	General notions of the organization of France. The duties and rights of citizens; compulsory education; military service, taxation, universal suffrage. The commune, the mayor and the municipal council.	More thorough study of the political, administrative and judicial organization of France. The Constitution, the President of the Republic, the Senate, the Chamber of Deputies, the law; central, departmental and communal administra-

7. Number, arithmetic.	First elements of notation and numeration. Simple exercises in mental calculation. Addition and subtraction of concrete numbers not exceeding 100. Study of the numbers from one to ten and of the expressions half, third, quarter. The four operations with numbers of two figures. The meter, the franc, the liter.	Principles of notation and numeration. Mental calculation. The four rules applied intuitively to the numbers from one to ten; then from one to twenty; then from one to 100. Study of the tables of addition and multiplication. Written calculation; addition, subtraction, multiplication; general rules of the three operations with whole numbers. Division limited to numbers of two figures in the divisor. Simple oral or written problems on common subjects; reasoning exercises on problems and on operations. Notions of the meter, liter, franc, gramme and of multiples and parts.	The department, the prefect and the general council. The State: Legislative, executive and judicial power.	tion, the different authorities; civil and penal courts; the different degrees of instruction; public force, the army.
			Review. The division of whole numbers. General idea of fractions. Decimal fractions. Application of the four rules to decimals. Rule of three, simple interest. Legal systems of weights and measures. Problems and practical exercises; reasoned solutions. Continuation and development of mental calculation as applied to all these operations.	Review with development, on one hand, for theory and reasoning; on the other, for rapid processes in mental and written calculation. Prime numbers. Most important characters of divisibility; principle of the division of a number into its prime factors; greatest common divisor; reduction applied to problems in interest, discount, partial payments, etc. The metric system, application to the measure of volumes and to their connections with weights. First notions of accounts.
8. Geometry		Simple exercises in recognizing and naming the most elementary regular figures; square, rectangle, triangle, circle. Different kinds of angles. Ideas of the three dimensions. Notions of solids by means of models. Frequent exercises in measurements and in comparison of the size of objects at sight; approximate appreciation of distances and of their values in metric measures.	Study and graphic representation on blackboard of plane geometric figures and of their most simple combinations. Practical notions of the cube, the prism, the cylinder, the sphere, with their fundamental properties; applications to the metric system.	Summary notions of plane geometry and of the measure of volumes. *For the boys.*—Application to the most simple operations in carpentry. Ideas of leveling. First notions of geometric drawing, with the elements of perspective.

PART II.—INTELLECTUAL EDUCATION —(Continued).

	Infant course — 5 to 7.	Elementary course — 7 to 9.	Middle course — 9 to 11	Advanced course — 11 to 13
9. Ornamental drawing.	Combinations of lines. Representation of these combinations on slate and paper, with common and colored crayon; simple inventive designs on paper ruled in squares; reproduction of very simple drawings made by the teacher. Representation of the most simple common objects.	Straight lines and their division into equal parts. Comparison of lines with each other. Reproduction and comparison of angles. First principles of ornamental drawing. Circumferences, regular polygons, rosaces étoilées.	Free-hand drawing.—Common geometric curves: Ellipses, spirals, etc. Curves taken from the vegetable kingdom: Stems, leaves, flowers. Copy of plaster models representing simple ornaments in slight relief. First notions of geometric drawing and elements of perspective. Representation of geometric solids and of simple common objects, without and with shading. Geometric drawing.—Use (on blackboard) of instruments for making straight lines and circumferences: Rule, compass, square, and protractor. Limit instruction to a knowledge of the use of these instruments. Skill in the actual use thereof will be acquired in the advanced course.	Free-hand drawing.—Drawing from copy and from model of purely geometric ornaments: Moldings, ovolos, rais de coeur, perles, fret-work, etc. Drawing from copy and from model of ornaments, whose elements are taken from the vegetable kingdom: Leaves, flowers and fruits, palms, foliage, etc. Elementary notions of the styles of architecture given on the blackboard by the teacher (three lessons). Drawing of the human head: Its parts, its proportions. Geometric drawing.—Drawing on paper with the aid of instruments the geometric figures made in the middle course on the blackboard. Use of colors. Drawings, reproducing motives of decoration for plane surfaces or for those in slight relief: Pavements, floorings, glazing, panels, ceilings (in India ink and in color of some of these designs). Representation of geometric solids and of simple objects, such as common pieces of furniture, etc.
10. Common elements of the physical and natural sciences.	Elementary notions of the human body: hygiene (simple counsels); simple comparative study of animals	Graduated object-lessons (man, animals, vegetables, minerals). Observation of objects and	Elementary notions of the natural sciences. Man.—Summary description of the human body and	Notions of the natural sciences: review and extension of the course in the middle class.

105

(Object-lessons)			
known to the child; of plants used in industry or for food; of minerals in common use. Air. water (vapor, cloud, rain, snow, ice). Simple object-lessons, with the objects before the eyes and in the hands of pupils. Exercises and familiar talks by way of acquiring the first elements of common information (right and left; names of the days and of the months; distinction between animals, minerals and vegetables; the seasons), and with the special aim of encouraging habits of observing, comparing, questioning, and retaining. In order to fix in the mind and heart of the pupil the unity of impression of the various forms of instruction, the teacher should combine as far as possible in the same object-lesson the games, songs, drawing and morale. The order of the lessons should follow the seasons, so that nature herself may furnish the necessary material, thus leading the child to form the habits of observing, comparing and judging.	of common phenomena, with simple explanations. Summary notions of the transformation of raw materials (foods, tissues, papers, woods, minerals). Little collections made by pupils, especially in the course of school excursions.	of the principal functions of life. *Animals.*—Notions of the great divisions and of the subdivision of vertebrates into classes, with the aid of an animal taken as type of each group. *Plants.*—Studies, with chosen types, of the principal organs of the plant; notions of the grand divisions of the vegetable kingdom. Indication of useful and harmful plants (especially in school excursions). The three states of bodies. Notions touching air, water and combustion. Simple experimental demonstrations.	*Man.*—Notions of digestion, circulation, respiration, the nervous system, the organs of the senses. Practical hygienic counsels. Abuse of alcohol, tobacco, etc. *Animals.*—Important characteristics of the classification. Useful and harmful animals. *Plants.*—Essential parts of the plant, principal groups. Herborizations. *Minerals.*—Summary notions of the soil, rocks, fossils; Examples taken from the vicinity. Excursions and little collections. *First notions of physics.*—Weight. Lever. First principles of the equilibrium of liquids. Atmospheric pressure; barometer. Elementary notions of and simple experiments with heat, light, electricity, magnetism (thermometer, steam-engine, lightning-rod, telegraph, compass). *First notions of chemistry.*—Idea of simple and composite bodies; metals and common salts.

14

PART II.—INTELLECTUAL EDUCATION —(Concluded).

	Infant course—5 to 7.	Elementary course—7 to 9.	Middle course—9 to 11.	Advanced course—11 to 12.
11. Agriculture and horticulture.		First lessons in the school garden.	Notions, à propos of reading, object-lessons and promenades, of the principal soils, manures, agricultural works and implements (spade, mattock, plough, etc.).	More methodic notions of agricultural works and tools, drainage, natural and artificial manures, sowing and harvesting; domestic animals, agricultural accounts. Notions of horticulture: principal processes of growth of the most useful vegetables of the vicinity. Notions of arboriculture: grafting and budding.
12. Singing	Kindergarten songs. Songs in unison and in two parts, learned exclusively by ear.	Songs learned at first exclusively by ear. Reading of notes.	Songs in unison and in two parts, learned by ear. knowledge of notes, staff, key of sol, reading, first exercises in intonation; value of notes, rondo, minim, crotchet, quaver, rests, measures in two, three and four time; reading of notes in beating the time. Simple exercises in solfège: oral dictation.	Continuation of the middle course. Intonation exercises. Key of sol and key of fa. Diatonic major scale, intervals and tone relations. Principal major and minor scales. Exercises in solfège, oral dictation, execution of pieces in unison and in two parts.

PART III.—MORAL EDUCATION.

1. Morale	Simple talks in connection with all class exercises and recreations. Short poems explained and learned by heart. Stories with a moral, told by teacher and followed by questions to bring out the points and to make sure that the children understand. Little songs. Particular attention of teacher toward children in whom she has observed	Familar talks. Readings with explanations (stories, examples, precepts, parables and fables). Memorizing. Practical exercises tending to put the *morale* in action in the class: 1. By close observation of character, studying the dispositions of the children in order to correct their faults or develop their qualities. 2. By the intelligent applica-	Talks, readings with explanations, practical exercises. Same manner of instruction as before, with a little more method and precision. Coordinate the lessons and readings so as not to leave untouched any important point in the following program: I. *The child in the family. Duties toward parents and grand-*	Talks, readings, practical exercises on the two preceding courses. A regular course of lessons, of which the number and the order may vary, in an elementary instruction in morals in general and social morals in particular, after the following program: 1. *The family.*—Duties of parents and children: reciprocal duties of masters and

tion of school discipline as a means of education. Distinguish carefully between failure and the simple infraction of a rule; show the relation of the fault to the penalty; be perfectly just in the government of the class; inspire contempt for tale-bearing, dissimulation and hypocrisy; place frankness and right above everything, encouraging freedom of speech by attending to the reclamations, demands, etc. of the children.

3. By appealing constantly to the feelings and to the moral judgment of the child.
(Let the children be often the judges of their own conduct; lead them to esteem moral and intellectual effort.)

4. By the correction of foolish notions (prejudices and popular superstitions, belief in witches, in ghosts, in the influence of certain numbers, in foolish fears, etc.).

5. By lessons drawn from facts observed by the children themselves. Lead them to feel the sad consequences of the vices which come under their notice: drunkenness, sloth, disorder, cruelty, brutal appetites, etc. Inspire the children with as much compassion for the victims of the evil as horror for the evil itself; proceed in the same way by concrete examples and by appeals to the immediate experience of the children in order to develop moral

some fault or some budding vice.

parents.—Obedience, respect, love, gratitude. To aid parents in their work; to comfort them in sickness; to take care of them in old age.
Duties of brothers and sisters.—To love one another; protection of the younger by the elder; force of example.
Duties toward servants.—To treat them kindly and politely.
The child in school.—Assiduity, docility, work, convenance.
Duties toward the teacher.
Duties toward comrades.
The country.—France, her greatness and her misfortunes.
Duties toward the native country and toward society.

II.

Duties toward self.—The body: cleanliness and temperance; evils of drunkenness; gymnastics.
Les biens extérieurs.—Economy; avoidance of debts; effects of the passion for gambling; moderation in desire for money and gain; prodigality, avarice.
Work. (Never lose time, general obligation to work, dignity of manual labor.)
The Soul.—Veracity and sincerity; never tell a lie. Personal dignity, self-respect. Modesty; not to be blind to one's faults. Shun pride, vanity, coquetry, frivolity. To be ashamed of ignorance and of idleness. Courage in danger, and in misfortune, patience, initiative spirit. Dangers of wrath. Treat animals kindly; do not make them suffer needlessly.

servants: the family spirit.
2. *Society.*—Necessity and benefits of society, justice, solidarity, fraternity.
Applications and developments of the idea of justice: respect for human life and liberty, respect for property, respect for promises, respect for the honor and reputation of others.—Probity, equity, loyalty, delicacy. Respect for opinions and beliefs.
Applications and developments of the idea of charity or of fraternity. Forms of charity, duties of benevolence, of gratitude, of tolerance, of clemency, etc. Devotion; show that there is opportunity for devotion in every day life.
3. *The country.*—What one owes one's country (obedience to the laws, military service, discipline, devotion, fidelity to the flag). Taxes (condemnation of all fraud against the State). The vote (it is morally obligatory, it ought to be free, conscientious, disinterested, intelligent. Rights which correspond to these duties: personal freedom, liberty of conscience, liberty of work, liberty of association. Guaranty of security of life and property. The national sovereignty. Explanation of the *devise* of the Republic: "Liberty, equality, fraternity." In each chapter of the course in social morals, the teacher is to call the attention of the child, without metaphysical discussions, to

1. The distinction between

PART III.—MORAL EDUCATION—(Concluded).

Infant course—5 to 7.	Elementary course—7 to 9.	Middle course—9 to 11.	Advanced course—11 to 13.
	feelings: *e. g.* create a feeling of admiration for universal order and for religious sentiment by causing the children to contemplate grand natural scenery; the feeling of charity, by pointing out some misery to be assisted, by giving them an opportunity to do some charitable act; the feelings of gratitude and sympathy by the recital of a courageous act, by a visit to some philanthropic institution, etc.	Law Gramont, protective societies for animals. *Duties toward man.*—Justice and charity (the golden rule). Injure no one's life, person, property, or reputation. Goodness, fraternity. Tolerance, respect for the faith of others. N.B.: Throughout this course the teacher begins with the existence of conscience, of the moral law and of obligation. He appeals to the sentiment and to the idea of duty and responsibility. He never enters on theoretic demonstrations. *Duties toward God.*—The teacher is not called on to give a course *ex professo* on the nature and attributes of God; the instruction which he should give all without distinction is limited to two points: 1. The children are taught not to pronounce lightly the name of God. The teacher associates closely with the idea of the first cause and of the Perfect Being a sentiment of respect and veneration: he accustoms each child to surround the idea of God with the same respect, although it may be presented to him in forms different from those of his own religion.	duty and interest, even when they seem to clash, that is to say, the imperative and disinterested character of duty; 2. The distinction between the written and the moral law: the one fixes a minimum of prescriptions which society imposes on all her members under fixed penalties, the other imposes on each, in the secret of his conscience a duty which no one compels him to perform, but which he can not neglect without feeling culpable toward himself and toward God.

2. Without occupying himself with special prescriptions of the various religious beliefs, the teacher attempts to make the child understand and feel that his first duty is to God, that is, obedience to God's laws as revealed by conscience and reason.

TIME-TABLES IN LOWER PRIMARY SCHOOLS.

I.

SCHOOLS IN WHICH THE THREE COURSES ARE SEPARATE, OR THOSE IN WHICH THE MIDDLE AND ADVANCED COURSES ALONE ARE TOGETHER.

ELEMENTARY COURSE

Morning.

8.30 to 9.00... Moral or civic instruction.
9.00 to 9.30... Reading.
9.30 to 10.00... Arithmetic or metric system.
10.00 to 10.15... Recess.
10.15 to 11.00... French.
11.00 to 11.30... Writing.

Afternoon.

1.00 to 1.30... History or geography.
1.30 to 2.00... Reading.
2.00 to 2.30... Drawing, manual training, military exercises.
2.30 to 2.45... Recess.
2.45 to 3.15... Writing.
3.15 to 4.00... Object-lessons and singing.

MIDDLE AND ADVANCED COURSES.

Morning.

8.30 to 9.00... Moral or civic instruction.
9.00 to 10.00... Arithmetic, metric system, geometry.
10.00 to 10.15... Recess.
10.15 to 11.00... French.
11.00 to 11.30... Writing (middle course), composition (advanced course).

Afternoon.

1.00 to 2.00... History or geography.
2.00 to 2.30... Reading; memory exercises.
2.30 to 2.45... Recess.
2.45 to 3.30... Drawing, singing, manual training or composition.
3.30 to 4.00... Physical and natural sciences; agriculture and horticulture.

II.

UNGRADED SCHOOLS.

Elementary course.

8.30 to 9.00... Moral and civic instruction.
9.00 to 10.00... Reading, arithmetic or metric system.
10.00 to 10.15... Recess.
10.15 to 11.00... Various exercises in language and grammar.
11.00 to 11.30... Writing.
1.00 to 2.00... Reading, talks on history and geography.
2.00 to 2.30... Writing.
2.30 to 2.45... Recess.
2.45 to 3.30... Drawing, singing, and manual training.
3.30 to 4.00... Object-lessons or reading.

Middle and advanced courses.

8.30 to 9.00...	Moral and civic instruction.
9.00 to 10.00...	Arithmetic, metric system, geometry.
10.00 to 10.15...	Recess.
10.15 to 11.00...	French.
11.00 to 11.30...	Writing.
1.00 to 2.00...	History or geography.
2.00 to 2.30...	Reading; memory exercises.
2.30 to 2.45...	Recess.
2.45 to 3.30...	Drawing, singing, and manual training.
3.30 to 4.00...	Physical and natural sciences; agriculture and horticulture.

TWENTY-FIRST CHAPTER.

UPPER PRIMARY SCHOOLS AND COURS COMPLÉMENTAIRES.

Establishments for upper primary instruction take the name *cours complémentaires* if annexed to primary schools and under the same direction. They are called upper primary schools if in a separate building and under other direction.

The duration of the course in the *cours complémentaires* is not to exceed two years. There are two divisions of the pupils, which may be united under one teacher.

The course in upper primary schools is at least two years in length. These schools are full course (*de plein exercice*) if the course is three years or more in length.

No pupil may be received either in an upper primary school or in a complementary course who does not hold the certificate of primary studies (page 54).

The complementary courses should have separate class-rooms. The upper primary school should have as many class-rooms as there are years in the course of study. It should have a room for instruction in drawing, a gymnasium and a department for manual training.

The course of study in *cours complémentaires* and upper primary schools is given below (page 113).

During the first three years of upper primary instruction, there should be six hours of class-work daily (Sundays and Thursdays excepted). The weekly division of time should be about as follows: Nine hours for literary instruction (morals, civics, the French language, history and geography); nine hours for scientific instruction (mathematics, physical and natural science); four hours for the modern languages; three hours for drawing; four hours for manual training; one hour for music.

Gymnastic and military exercises should be held outside these hours of class-work.

In the fourth year of upper primary instruction and later, the time devoted to manual training and to technical instruction may be increased, but at least ten hours weekly should be reserved for the other subjects.

Instruction in drawing, music, modern languages, gymnastics and manual training should be confided, as far as possible, to teachers attached to the school.

Pupils seeking admission to upper primary schools must take the entrance examination as the basis of classification.

The regulations for holidays, vacations, discipline, the construction and furnishing of school buildings, etc., correspond very closely with those enforced in lower primary schools.

Pupils more than 18 years of age are not permitted to frequent the upper primary schools.

Écoles maternelles, lower and upper primary schools and normal schools are gratuitous.

Scholarships are awarded annually to the best pupils in the upper primary schools. They are good for three school years and the time may be extended to four years. These scholarships pay the whole or a portion of the living expenses of the holders in France, or permit them to study in a foreign country.

The upper primary schools referred to in this chapter do not include the technical or manual training schools, but only those which are under the sole charge of the minister of public instruction.

The statistics for 1887 show that 56 per cent of the graduates of these schools devoted themselves to agriculture, commerce or industry, and 17 per cent entered higher schools.

In 1884, including the 320 complementary courses, there were 559 of these establishments, of which 419 were for boys, and 140 for girls; 539 were public schools.

In 1887, including the 431 complementary courses, there were 733 of these establishments, of which 510 were for boys, and 223 for girls; 686 were public schools. Two hundred and five boys and 76 girls' complementary courses were for one year; the rest for two years. Eighty-three schools for boys and 30 for girls had a two years' course; 101 schools for boys and 41 for girls had a three years' course.

In 1887, 10,052 pupils attended the complementary courses, which were all public; 20,673 attended the public and 7,716 the private schools.

OFFICIAL PROGRAMS OF INSTRUCTION IN UPPER PRIMARY SCHOOLS AND COURS COMPLÉMENTAIRES.

PHYSICAL EDUCATION AND PREPARATION FOR PROFESSIONAL APPRENTICESHIP.

1. GYMNASTICS.

Complementary courses.—Continuation of the exercises of the advanced course in lower primary schools. Follow the special manuals for each sex, published by the ministry.
Upper primary schools.—Movements in a body. Exercises with apparatus.

2. MILITARY EXERCISES FOR THE BOYS.

Complementary courses.—Continuation of the exercises of the advanced course in lower primary schools.
Upper primary schools.—Military drill: Review without arms. Formation in open order. Military and topographic marches. Exercises preparatory to target-practice. Practical study of the mechanism of the gun. Conform with the special manual published by the ministries of public instruction and of war.

3. MANUAL TRAINING FOR THE BOYS.

Complementary courses.—Same as in the upper primary schools.
Upper primary schools.—Wood-working. Principal woods used in structures or in machines. Their qualities and uses. Principal tools employed in working wood. Sawing, boring, planing, turning, joining, iron-working. Properties, varieties, qualities and uses of iron. Principal tools used usually in working iron. Filing, hammering, forging, soldering, engraving, drilling, turning, joining, adjusting. Working drawings of simple objects, and construction of the objects from the drawings.

4. MANUAL TRAINING FOR THE GIRLS.

Complementary courses.—Same as in the upper primary schools with less development.
Upper primary schools.—In the following divisions:

a. *Housekeeping.*

Organization and maintenance of the household.
Heating. Lighting.
Maintenance of the furniture.
Care of clothing and linen.
Washing. Wash-house. Ironing.
Flour. Baking. Furnace. Bread-baking. Pastry-work.
Household provisions. Wood. Coal. Drinking-water.
Wine and its care. Vinegar.
Cider. Beer. Coffee. Oil. Grease. Sugar.
Preservation and cooking of meat.
Qualities and choice of meats.
Elementary principles of the *cuisine*.
Kettle. Broth. Frying. Roasting.
Game. Fish.
Preservation and cooking of vegetables.
Preservation of fruits. Fruit-garden. Packing and transportation of fruits.
Manufacture of preserves, brandied fruits, syrups, *liqueurs*.
Household accounts.
N. B.— The pupils should have as much practical household work as possible at home.

b. *Gardening.*

Summary notions of agriculture.—Soil, manures and improvements. Different kinds of husbandry.

Garden.—General arrangement; paths, borders, walls, garden works and tools.

Fruit-garden.—General principles of the culture of fruit trees, with application to the varieties best suited to the district. Diseases among fruit-trees. Destruction of harmful insects.

Kitchen-garden.—Varieties, culture and harvesting of vegetables. Harvesting and preservation of grains. Forced cultivation: hotbeds, cold-frames, plant-protectors.

Notions of floriculture.—Flowers cultivated for ornament and for the manufacture of perfumery.

c. *Farming.*

Farm.—Cow-house and dairy. General notions of the manufacture of butter and cheese.

Summary notions of the sheep-fold and of the keeping of hogs. Poultry-yard. Rearing and fattening of poultry. Pigeons. Rabbits. Bees and silk-worms.

d. *Sewing.*

Different stitches. Darning. Knitting. Patching.

Joining and setting together. Linen. *Chemises* and shirts for men and boys. Pantaloons, waistcoats, bonnets, etc.

Cutting and making articles of clothing. Study of patterns. Princess robe. Basque. Clothing for children.

N. B.—The various parts of this program should be developed according to the needs of the locality.

INTELLECTUAL EDUCATION.

1. READING.

Complementary courses.—Exercises in reading aloud, with explanation; exercises in elocution and in pronunciation. Reading aloud by teacher and pupils, with explanation and analysis; recitation; exercises in diction in connection with classic texts.

2. WRITING.

Complementary courses.—Running hand, round hand, *bâtarde*, commercial hand.

Upper primary schools.—Running hand, round hand, *bâtarde*, commercial hand, caligraphy.

3. FRENCH LANGUAGE AND ELEMENTS OF LITERATURE.

Complementary courses.—Review of the advanced course in lower primary schools. Continuation of the same exercises with a little more development.

Oral exercises, accounts stated and explained aloud, dictations and grammatical exercises on the essential rules of syntax, and especially reading aloud by teacher and pupils, with explanations.

Upper primary schools.—Review and development of the advanced course in lower primary schools. Methodic review of syntax; formation of words, families of words. Exercises in distinguishing synonyms. Exercises on the proposition. Coordination and subordination of the members of sentences.

Elementary principles of composition; application of these principles to narrations letters, reports, etc.

Elementary notions of the history of French literature. Pupils are to be exercised, in writing business letters and compositions graduated in point of difficulty, in describing objects previously examined under the direction of the teacher, in summing up a selection in reading or a lesson in discussing an historic judgment or a moral thought, etc. Pupils are to have practical oral exercises similar to those in writing referred to above.

4. HISTORY.

Complementary courses.—Methodic review of the history of France; formation of the precinct of jurisdiction; progress of national institutions; great events of modern times.

Upper primary schools.—Rivalry between France and England; hundred years' war. The Turks in Europe; fall of Constantinople.
Great inventions; mariner's compass, powder, paper, printing. Discovery of the new world.
Charles VII and Louis XI. The wars in Italy.
Francis I.—Struggle between France and Austria. The *Renaissance.*
The Reformation and religious wars.
Henry IV.—The edict of Nantes; Sully.
Richelieu and Mazarin.—Treaties of Westphalia and of the Pyrenees.
Louis XIV.—Wars and conquests. Revocation of the edict of Nantes. Colbert, Louvois. Vauban. Arts and letters in the seventeenth century.
Louis XV.—The Regency; the system of law. Decline of the French power; rise of Prussia and of Russia; maritime struggle between France and England; the Indies and Canada. Philosophers and economists.
Louis XVI.—Turgot, Necker. American war. Convocation of the *États généraux.* Formation of French territory under the ancient monarchy. Institutions before 1789. State of France in 1789 (the royal power and the *États généraux*, the *Trois ordres*, corporations, privileges, justice, the army, taxes, agriculture, the colonies, etc.).
The Constituent Assembly, its reforms. The principles of 1789. Constitution of 1791.
The Legislative Assembly.
The Convention. Establishment of the Republic. The factions. Trial and death of Louis XVI. Wars. Treaty of Bâle. Institutions and creations of the Convention. Constitution of the year III.
The Directory. Bonaparte. The 18 *Brumaire.*
Constitution of the year VIII. The institutions of the Consulate. The civil code. The peace of Amiens.
The Empire. The continental blockade. The treaties of 1815.
The Restauration. The charter, the parliamentary *régime.* Capture of Algiers. The monarchy of July. The Republic of 1848. The Second Empire. The events of 1870; the treaty of Frankfurt. Constitutional laws.

5. GEOGRAPHY.

Complementary courses.— Physical and political geography of Europe; general study of the geography of other parts of the world; special study of the geography of France, of Algeria and of the French colonies; map-drawing from memory.

Upper primary schools.— The continents. Principal reliefs of the soil.
Oceans and their currents. Great river basins.
Asia, Africa, America, Oceanica. Principal countries.
European colonies. Staple productions.
Commercial relations of the five parts of the world with each other and especially with France.
Europe. General configuration. Mountain systems.
Distribution of water. Different climates.
European countries; languages, religions, governments.
Principal industrial and commercial centers. Ways of communication.
Relations of France with the different countries of Europe.
France. Configuration and extent. Boundaries.
Reliefs of the soil; mountains, plateaus and plains.
Water systems; declivities and basins; rivers and tributaries; lakes, ponds, swamps etc.
Political geography. Ancient provinces and departments.
Administrative divisions.

Economic geography. Zones of culture. Coal-fields.
Principal agricultural and industrial productions. Ways of communication; canals, highways, railways.
Algeria and the colonies.

6. Civics, Common Law and Notions of Political Economy.

Complementary courses.—Review of the advanced course in lower primary schools.
Upper primary schools.—Development of the program of the advanced course in lower primary schools.
More particular notions of the political, financial, administrative and judicial organization of France.
Elementary notions of civil law (the family and the civil state, the laws of property, inheritances, contracts) and of commercial law (merchants, commercial societies, bills of exchange, orders, checks).
General notions of political economy.
Production of wealth. Factors in production; material, work, economy, capital, property.
Circulation and distribution of wealth. Exchange, money, credit, wages and interest.
Consumption of wealth. Productive and unproductive consumption; the question of luxury; expenses of the State; taxes, the budget.

7. Arithmetic, Geometry, Surveying and Accounting.

Complementary courses.—Review and development of the course in lower primary schools.
Upper primary schools.—Under the following heads:

a. *Arithmetic.*

Operations with whole numbers. Short methods in oral and written work. Simple characters of divisibility. Proof by 9 of the multiplication and division. Greatest common divisor of two numbers. Decomposition of numbers into prime factors. Composition of the greatest common divisor and of the least common multiple of several numbers. Common fractions. Simplification of fractions. Reduction of fractions to a common denominator. Operations with fractions. Decimal fractions. Operations with decimal fractions. Reduction of common to decimal fractions. Square root. Practice in extracting the square root of numbers.
Simple notions of ratios and proportions. Proportional magnitudes.
Varied problems: Simple interest. Discount. Exchange. Public funds. Stocks. Obligations. Insurance. Banking. Partnership. Taxes. Alligation.

b. *Metric system.*

Numerous applications, principally to the measure of surfaces and of simple volumes.

c. *Algebra.*

Elements of algebraic calculation.
Solution of numeric equations of the first degree with one and several unknown quantities.
Application to problems in arithmetic.
Solution of equations of the first degree. Problems and numeric exercises.
Solution of equations of the second degree with one unknown quantity; application to problems in arithmetic and geometry.
Principal properties of arithmetic and geometric progressions.
General ideas of logarithms. Use of logarithmic tables with four or five decimals.
Applications to compound interest and to annuities.

d. *Geometry.*

Plane geometry and its applications. General method employed in making a geometric plan. Use of instruments. Construction of plans. The scale. Simple topographic problems.
Elementary notions of solid geometry, with applications. Elements of trigonometry, with the most common applications.

e. *Surveying*.

Practical exercises in surveying. Computations from maps. Problems in surveying. Land registration. Leveling. Use of the water level. Sighting. Reading of topographic charts.

f. *First notions of business and of accounting*.

Merchants. Business transactions. Purchases and sales. Memoranda. Invoices. Receipts. Simple bills. Bills payable to order. Bills of exchange. Indorsement. Acceptance. Protest. Drafts. Checks. Negotiation of commercial paper. Discount. Commission. Bookkeeping. Notions of single-entry bookkeeping. Insufficiency of the method of single entry. Double-entry bookkeeping. Failure. Arrangement with creditors. Rehabilitation. Bankruptcy.

8. ELEMENTS OF THE PHYSICAL SCIENCES.

Complementary courses.— First notions of physics and of chemistry, taught essentially by means of simple experiments and elementary explanations.
Weight; its effects; lever; scales.
Pressure exerted by liquids.
Atmospheric pressure, barometer.
Simple experiments in heat, light, electricity, magnetism (thermometer, steam engine, lightning-rod, telegraph, mariner's compass).
Ideas of simple bodies, of composite bodies. Metals and common salts.
Upper primary schools.— Under the heads:

a. *Physics*.

Usual notions on the three states of bodies, the properties of liquids and gases, atmospheric pressure, the barometer.
Experimental notions on the effects of heat, the thermometer, wind, rain, snow; on the principal electric phenomena, the lightning-rod.
Equilibrium of liquids, communicating vessels.
Hydraulic press, floating bodies, use of areometers.
Mariotte's law. Manometers. Pumps. Siphon.
Expansion of bodies by heat. Applications. Conductivity and applications.
Sources of heat. Heating of solids or liquids and of the air of dwellings and shops.
Changes of state: Fusion, evaporation, boiling, distillation. Use of steam as a motive force. Electric phenomena. Batteries, applications of electricity, electric light, telegraphy.
Magnets, use of the mariner's compass. Electro-magnets.
Production of sound. Echo.
Reflection of light, plane mirror, concave mirror.
Lenses; uses of the magnifying glass, of the microscope, of spectacles.
Notions of physical mechanics. Motions. Forces. Idea of the working of forces.
Steam motors.
Industrial applications suited to the locality.

b. *Chemistry*.

Exercises in observation and examination of familiar facts introductory to the study of chemistry.
Water, air, their importance in geology and in animal and vegetable life. Simple experiments on the properties of water and of air. Analysis and synthesis of water.
Metalloids and the most useful metals.
Oxygen. Hydrogen. Nitrogen. Sulphur. Chlorine. Phosphorus. Carbon. Iron. Zinc. Tin. Lead. Copper. Mercury. Silver. Gold. Platinum.
Notions of acids, oxides and salts.
Notions of organic chemistry: *From an industrial standpoint:* Illuminating gas. Benzine. Turpentine. Petroleum. Soap. The candle. Starch. Sugar. Manufacture of alcohols. Paper. Natural and artificial coloring matter. Dyeing. Preservation of wood. Tanning.

From an agricultural standpoint: Manufacture of bread. Fermented *liqueurs* (wine, beer, cider). Cheeses. Composition of foods. Eggs. Milk. Blood. Flesh. Preservation of alimentary articles.

Chemical laws. Notions of equivalents, of the composition of bodies in weight and volume.

Principal industrial applications.

9. ELEMENTS OF THE NATURAL SCIENCES.

Complementary courses. Review with extension of the advanced course in lower primary schools.

Upper primary schools. Elementary notions of the human organization.

Enumeration of the principal organs and their functions.

Functions of nutrition. Functions of relation. Notions of domestic animals and cultivated plants of the locality.

Useful and harmful animals and plants, especially those found in France and in the locality.

The most common and useful minerals of the country.

Classification of animals. Elementary study of vertebrates, dwelling particularly on domestic animals. Mammals and their principal orders. Birds, nesting and migrations; insectivorous species. Scaly reptiles. Batracians and their metamorphoses. Fish, common alimentary species of salt and fresh water.

Invertebrates. Summary study of insects and their metamorphoses. Indication of the principal, useful and harmful species of the neighborhood. Summary notions of the mollusca, principally those which serve for food and industry.

Notions of the functions of vegetables and of their classification. Indication of the most important vegetables.

Notions of geology. Study chiefly the geology of the locality. Common phenomena. Brief notice of the composition and structure of rocks; of geologic forces; of historic geology.

Hygiene. Advice relative to the care of the body; nourishment, clothing, heating, lighting.

Advice touching the best sanitary conditions of the home; quarters of domestic animals.

Public hygiene: Rural sanitary conditions, irrigation, drainage, draining of swamps. Salubrity of cities, sewers and water-closets; work-shops, factories, wood-yards. First steps to take in cases of accident while awaiting the arrival of a physician. Precautions to take in case of epidemics.

10. AGRICULTURE AND HORTICULTURE.

Complementary courses.—Same program as in upper primary schools, but with less development.

Upper primary schools.—Practical notions of vegetation, of the growth of vegetables of their different modes of reproduction (grains, slips, grafting), of the nature of different soils, of manures and their proper use, of fallowing.

Knowledge and use of agricultural implements. Principal agricultural machines.

Principal operations of agriculture: Clearing, planting, transplanting, drainage, irrigation.

Principal agricultural products of France and particularly of the locality (cereals, alimentary roots and tubers, fodder, oleaginous and textile plants, grape-culture).

Diseases of plants and remedies; parasitic vegetables.

Vegetables, fruits and flowers. Use of green-houses.

Care of fruit trees.

Care of domestic animals. Culture of bees.

11. DRAWING.

Complementary courses.—Continuation of primary instruction, with application of the following program:

Free-hand drawing. Drawing, from copy and model, of purely geometric ornaments: Moldings, ovolo , *rais de cœur, perles,* fretwork, etc.

Drawing, from copy and model, of ornaments whose elements are taken from the vegetable kingdom; leaves, flowers and fruits, palms, foliage.

Exercises in drawing from memory.

Elementary ideas of the styles of architecture given on the blackboard by the teacher (three lessons).

Drawing of the human head; its parts, its proportions.

Geometric drawing. Execution on paper, with the aid of instruments, of geometric figures which have been drawn on the blackboard in the middle course.

Use of colors.

Drawings reproducing decorative motives for plane surfaces or those in feeble relief: Pavements, floorings, glazings, panels, ceilings.

Drawings in India ink and in color of some of these designs.

Representation of geometric solids and of simple objects, such as ordinary pieces of furniture, etc. Use of colors to express the nature of materials. Coloring of plans and charts.

Upper primary schools.— Same program as for the complementary courses.

Directions furnished by the *Administration des Beaux-arts* to fix the mean of this course, and, consequently, that of the examinations.

GEOMETRIC DRAWING.

a. Figures in plane geometry.

To execute at a fixed scale, after a given design, a decorative motive for a plane surface (pavements, flooring, glazing.)

To color the different parts either according to the directions given in the design or in some other manner, producing a pleasing effect.

b. Projection.

To execute at a fixed scale, after a given design, the drawing by horizontal projection (plan) and by vertical projection (elevation) of a geometric solid.

To shift this solid as directed and to give the new projections.

c. Penetration.

To execute at a fixed scale, after a given design, the drawing by projection (plan, elevation) of two solids which penetrate.

The development of the surfaces of the solids is to be given if they are susceptible of development.

NOTE.—These cases of penetration are to be very simple. The number is to be limited and the application is to be pointed out at once. Examples: sphere and regular prism (square or hexagonal) whose axis passes through the center of the sphere. (Application to the drawing of nuts and screws). Cylinders of the same diameter (application to an elbowed pipe), etc.

d. Perspective.

To represent, by linear perspective, simple solids (cube, prism, cylinder), isolated, juxtaposited or superposited but not penetrating.

The pupils are to receive a design on which the dimensions of the solids are given· their respective positions, and the point of view, as well as the dimensions of the perspective drawing.

e. Designs.

Parts of machines and plans of buildings:

To execute at a fixed scale, after a design, the drawing of a part of a machine or of a plan of a building.

Ornamental drawing.

a. These drawings are always from models.

b. The conditions and the rules for the correction of the drawings are determined in the decree of May 1, 1883.

12. SINGING.

Complementary courses.—Continuation of the exercises of the lower primary school.
Upper primary schools.—Exercises of diction, of intonation and of time.
Singing of a melody with words.
Execution of choruses in several parts.
Study of *solfège*: Knowledge of the signs, of the intervals, of the tones, of the changes, of the measures, of the rhythms and of the keys.
Reading at sight of a lesson of *solfège* in keys of *sol*, *fa* and *ut*.
Musical dictation with transposition of keys.
General principles of music.

13. MODERN LANGUAGES.

Complementary courses.—As in the upper primary schools.
Upper primary schools.—Reading and writing. Translations and explanations. Practical notions of grammar. Conversation on a subject taken from every-day life from manual training, from number, from the life of plants and animals, from voyages, etc. Written translation at sight of simple sentences chosen in the same way. Questions on words or constructions used in the exercises. Oral and written exercises. Simple compositions, business letters, etc.

MORAL EDUCATION.

Complementary courses.—Instruction is of the same character as in the lower primary schools. It is essentially practical and experimental. Its object is to form and exercise the moral sense of the pupil.

The methods of instruction are conversations, and practical exercises tending to put into action what has been learned. In addition thereto the course comprises a regular series of lessons forming the methodic review of the studies of the middle and advanced classes in the lower primary school. These lessons follow the program given below:

a. The family.—Duties of parents and children; reciprocal duties of masters and servants; family spirit;

b. Society.—Necessity and benefits of society, justice, solidarity, fraternity.

Applications and developments of the ideas of justice: Respect for human life and liberty, respect for property, respect for promises, respect for the honor and reputation of others. Probity, equity, loyalty, delicacy. Respect for opinions and beliefs.

Applications and developments of the idea of charity or of fraternity. Its different degrees; duties of benevolence, tolerance, clemency, etc. Devotion, the supreme form of charity; show that it has a place in every-day life.

c. The country.—What man owes his country (obedience to the laws, military service, discipline, devotion, fidelity to the flag, etc.). Taxation (condemnation of all fraud toward the State). The vote (it is morally obligatory; it ought to be free, conscientious, disinterested, intelligent). Rights which correspond to those duties: Personal liberty, liberty of conscience, liberty of work, liberty of association. Guaranty of the security of the life and of the property of all. The national sovereignty. Explanation of the republican *devise*: "Liberty, equality, fraternity." In each chapter of this course in social morals, without entering into metaphysical discussions, the attention of the pupil is to be called to:

1. The difference between duty and interest even when they seem to be the same, *i. e.*, the imperative and disinterested character of duty;

2. The distinction between the written and the moral law: The one fixes a minimum of prescriptions which society imposes on all her members under fixed penalties; the other imposes on each one in the secret of his conscience a duty which no one compels him to fulfil, but which he can not neglect without feeling guilty toward himself, toward society and toward God.

Upper primary schools.—Under the following divisions: Preliminary notions. Moral responsibility. Liberty. Duty. Right. Virtue.

Domestic duties.—Duties of children toward parents, of brothers and sisters toward each other, mutual duties of husbands and wives, of masters and servants, duties of parents toward children. Family spirit.

Civic duties.—The country, the State and the citizen.
Public authority, the constitution and the laws.
Duties of citizens: Obedience to the laws, military service, taxation, voting.
Duties of the governing: The great public powers.
Patriotism.
Duties of nations toward each other.—Notions of international rights.
General duties of social life.—Respect for person, life, liberty, honor, reputation, opinions and beliefs, property, etc.; respect for contracts and promises; distributive and remunerative justice; equity.
Charity, benevolence, alms-giving, goodness, solidarity, politeness.
Duties toward animals.
Personal duties.—Self-respect, veracity, modesty, foresight, courage, self-control.
Development of all our faculties; work.
Religious duties and corresponding privileges.—Place of religious sentiment in *morale*.
Liberty of worship.
Sanctions of *morale*, virtue making happy. God and the future life.

TWENTY-SECOND CHAPTER.

SCHOOLS FOR INDUSTRIAL AND COMMERCIAL TRAINING.

These schools are classed with the public primary schools, and are regulated by the law of December 11, 1880, and by the decree of March 17, 1888. The course of study covers at least three years.

Schools for industrial and commercial training (*écoles manuelles d'apprentissage*, and *écoles primaires supérieures préparatoires au commerce ou à l'industrie*) assure pupils:

1. A complement of primary instruction.
2. Industrial or commercial instruction, or both.

The time-tables in these schools are divided as follows:

INDUSTRIAL SCHOOLS AND CLASSES.

GENERAL PLAN OF INSTRUCTION.	FIRST YEAR.	SECOND YEAR.	THIRD YEAR.
	Hours daily.	Hours daily.	Hours daily.
Primary instruction	2 hours	2 hours	2 hours.
Manual training	3 hours	4 hours	5 hours.
Drawing	1 hour	1 hour	1 hour.
Scientific and technical instruction with industrial applications	1 hour	1 hour	1 hour.
Total hours of work	7 hours	8 hours	9 hours.

COMMERCIAL SCHOOLS AND CLASSES.

GENERAL PLAN OF INSTRUCTION.	FIRST YEAR. Hours daily.	SECOND YEAR. Hours daily.	THIRD YEAR. Hours daily.
Primary instruction	1 hour	1 hour	1 hour.
Commercial bureau	2 hours	3 hours	3 hours.
Commercial geography	1 hour	1 hour	1 hour.
Modern languages	2 hours	1 hour	2 hours.
Drawing	1 hour	1 hour	1 hour.
Total hours of work	7 hours	7 hours	8 hours.

Pupils under 12 are not admitted to these schools. They must hold the certificate of primary studies or its equivalent.

In schools for girls the working hours are reduced to six, for the first year; seven, for the second year; eight, for the third year.

In case a fourth year is added to the course, the time-table is determined by a special program.

OBSERVATION.

A commission appointed to make inquiry and report to the Legislature of Pennsylvania respecting industrial education made quite an elaborate report in 1889 on the condition of industrial education in France and in other countries. It was my good fortune to meet in Paris George W. Atherton, chairman of this commission, and to visit with him some of the leading French industrial schools. The report of the commission covers 592 pages and is very valuable to persons interested in this subject.

One of our most profitable visits was at the *École Diderot* in Paris which had at that time about 300 pupils.

The object of this school is to prepare workmen for eight of the principal trades. The apprenticeship lasts three years. During the first year pupils pass from one workshop to another in order to test their aptitude. At the close of this year they choose a trade with the concurrence of their parents, and devote the second and third years to this special apprenticeship. Pupils are paid for satisfactory work at a fixed scale. Two-thirds of their wages are allowed the pupils monthly, and one third is kept by the director until their graduation.

French schools in cities and centers of population are abundantly supplied with apparatus, and the teachers are remarkably ingenious in its use. The noticeable feature of the apparatus used in industrial schools is that much of it is made by the pupils. At the *École Diderot*, for example, the pupils lunch at the school, and the question of preparing and cooking potatoes has received attention. The director, who is remarkably ingenious, has invented two large machines, one for peeling and one for cooking potatoes. Both were made by the pupils, and both work to a charm.

TWENTY-THIRD CHAPTER.
PRIMARY NORMAL SCHOOLS.

Primary normal schools are establishments for training teachers for the public *écoles maternelles*, the lower and upper primary schools.* Normal schools are under the rector subject to the authority of the minister. They are boarding schools. Board and lodgings are free. Day students may be admitted on the recommendation of the rector and with the approval of the minister. The course of study is three years in length. A primary practice-school is annexed to each normal school. In addition, an *école maternelle* is attached to each normal school for females.

Normal school directors are appointed by the minister. They should be 30 years of age and should hold the certificate of capacity for the inspection of primary schools and for the direction of normal schools.

A steward with the title *économe* is attached to each normal school. In normal schools for males, the *économe* is charged with the instruction in bookkeeping; in normal schools for females, with the instruction in domestic economy as well. These *économes* may also give other instruction according to their qualifications.

Candidates for the position of steward should hold the *brevet supérieur* and the *certificat d'aptitude pédagogique*. They should be at least 21 years of age, and should have served an apprenticeship of one year under the steward of a normal school.

Instruction in normal schools is given by professors, assistants and special teachers appointed by the minister. The direction of practice primary schools and *écoles maternelles* is confided to a member of the normal school faculty.

---

*There are also two advanced normal schools (*Fontenay-aux-Roses* and *Saint Cloud*). These schools (the former for men, the latter for women) train normal school professors and professors of upper primary schools. They are gratuitous and the course of study covers three years. The normal school (*Pape-Carpantier*) at Versailles trains directresses for the *écoles maternelles*.

Workmen may be employed in normal schools for males to assist the professor of manual training.

In every normal school, receiving more than 60 pupils, the number of professors is fixed at five, not including the steward and director of the practice school (two for letters, three for the sciences and manual training). The number is fixed at four if the school has 60 pupils or less (two for letters, two for the sciences and manual training).

The summer vacation in normal schools is seven weeks in length. Holidays and other vacations correspond with those in primary sc ools. About five hours daily are devoted to meals, recreations and physical exercises, and eight hours to sleep.

STUDENTS.

The number of students each normal school may receive is fixed annually by the rector with the advice of the department council.

Candidates are:

1. To be between 16 and 18 years of age;
2. To hold the *brevet élémentaire*;
3. To place themselves under bond to serve 10 years in public instruction;
4. To be in a satisfactory physical condition.

The rector has authority to admit candidates more than 18 years of age.

The examination for admission is held before a commission appointed by the rector. The academy inspector is president of this commission. More than two trials are not authorized.

Candidates must submit birth certificate and biographic sketch. They are examined as to physical condition by the normal school physician.

Examinations for admission are both oral and written, including,—

1. An exercise in dictation of about twenty lines. The punctuation is not dictated, but candidates are allowed ten minutes in which to revise their work.

2. An exercise in penmanship (*bâtarde, ronde, cursive*, coarse, medium, fine). Three-quarters of an hour are given to this work.

3. A simple exercise in French composition (two hours).

4. The solution of one or more problems in arithmetic with explanation of processes (two hours).

5. An easy exercise in drawing (one and one-half hours).

6. Questions on the French language, arithmetic and the metric system, the history and geography of France, notions of general

geography, elementary notions of the physical and natural sciences (at least half an hour is devoted to each subject).

7. Abstracts of two lessons given by the professors on two subjects (one literary, the other scientific). These abstracts are to be prepared in half an hour each.

8. An exercise in music from the advanced course in primary schools.

9. Gymnastic exercises taken from the advanced course in primary schools; also, for the males, military exercises; for the females, needlework.

The examinations are divided into two parts. Only those candidates who succeed in passing the first part satisfactorily are admitted to the second. During the second series of tests, which are not to occupy more than one week, candidates are lodged and fed at the normal schools at the expense of their families.

Students leaving the normal schools voluntarily or excluded therefrom or breaking the engagement to serve 10 years in public instruction, must restore the cost of board, washing and books. Dispensations may be granted, however, by the minister on the recommendation of the rector and with the advice of professors and academy inspector.

Every normal graduate receives, when first called to a post of duty, an indemnity of twenty dollars.

Normal graduates are entitled to the first vacancies in public schools in accordance with their certificates of capacity.

Normal students have every opportunity for their religious duties.

The only punishments which are authorized are:

1. Detention within the school buildings.
2. Warning, pronounced by the director.
3. Public reprimand, pronounced according to the gravity of the offense by the director or by the academy inspector.
4. Suspension for a period not exceeding 15 days pronounced by the rector on the report of the academy inspector, and with the advice of the administrative council.*
5. Expulsion, pronounced by the minister on the recommendation of the rector.

---

* An administrative council, appointed for three years, and composed of the academy inspector as president, six members named by the rector, and two *counseillers généraux*, watches over the material interests of each normal school.

COURSE OF STUDY IN PRIMARY NORMAL SCHOOLS.

The following are abbreviated translations of the official time-tables and courses of study in primary normal schools for males and females, as published January 10, 1889:

NORMAL SCHOOLS FOR MALES.

SUBJECTS.	HOURS PER WEEK.		
	First year.	Second year.	Third year.
Literary instruction:			
Pyschology, morals, pedagogy	2	2	2
French language and literature	5	4	4
History and civics	3	3	3
Geography	1	1	1
Penmanship	2	1	
Modern languages	2	2	*2
Total	15	13	12
Scientific instruction:			
Mathematics	3	4	4
Physics and chemistry	2	2	3
Natural sciences and hygiene	1	1	†1
Drawing and modeling	4	4	4
Theoretic agriculture		1	1
Total	10	12	13
Manual and agricultural training	5	5	5
Military and gymnastic exercises	3	3	3
Music	2	2	2

* In addition to the two hours, one hour weekly is devoted to conversational exercises in the language studied.
† Hygiene and geology in the third year occupy together one hour weekly. Hygiene — twenty lessons.

NORMAL SCHOOLS FOR FEMALES.

SUBJECTS.	HOURS PER WEEK.		
	First year.	Second year.	Third year.
Literary instruction:			
Psychology, morals, pedagogy	2	2	2
French language and literature	5	4	4
History and civics	3	3	3
Geography	1	1	1
Penmanship	2	1	
Modern languages	2	2	*2
Total	15	13	12
Scientific instruction:			
Mathematics	2	2	2
Physics		1	1
Chemistry		1	1
Natural sciences and hygiene	1	1	1
Domestic economy			1
Drawing	4	4	4
Total	7	9	10
Needlework	3	2	2
Household duties and work in garden	2	2	2
Gymnastics	2	2	2
Music	2	2	2

* In addition to the two hours, one hour weekly is devoted to conversational exercises in the language studied.

NORMAL SCHOOLS FOR MALES.

FIRST YEAR.
I. Elementary Notions of Psychology.

Object of psychology.—Its relations to pedagogy and morals. General description of the human faculties.
Physical activity. –Movements, instincts, habits.
Sensibility. — Pleasure and pain. Physical sensibility: Needs and appetites. Moral sensibility: Family spirit; social and patriotic feelings; sentiment of the true, the beautiful, the good; religious feeling. Passion.
Intelligence.—Conscience; the senses; natural and acquired perceptions. Memory and imagination. Attention, abstraction and generalization ; judgment and reasoning. The principles of reason.
Will.—Liberty; habit.
Conclusions of psychology.—Duality of human nature. Spirit and body; moral, intellectual and animal life.

II. Application of Psychology to Education.

Physical education.—General health; children's games and exercises.
Intellectual education.—Development of the intellectual faculties at different ages; application to various forms of information. Education of the senses; simple observation exercises. Training of memory and imagination; judgment and reasoning. Different processes; induction ; deduction.
Methods of instruction.—Particular study of processes applicable to each subject.
Moral education.—Natural diversity in instincts and characters, modification of characters and formation of habits. Culture of sensibility of child. Education of the will. Discipline, rewards and punishments, emulation.

SECOND YEAR.
Theoretic Morals. Principles.

Introduction.—Object of *morale.*
Conscience.—Instinctive discernment of good and evil, development through education.
Liberty and responsibility.—Conditions, degrees and limitations of responsibility.
Obligation and duty.—Nature of moral law. Insufficiency of personal interest as basis of moral law. Insufficiency of sentiment.
Le bien and le devoir pur.—Dignity of man.
Sanctions of morale.—Relations between virtue and happiness. Individual sanctions. Social sanctions. Supreme sanctions: God and the future life.

Practical Morals. Applications.

Personal duties.— Their foundation. Self-respect, temperance, prudence, courage, respect for truth, promises, etc.
Family duties.—The family; its moral and social importance. Domestic duties.
General social duties.—Personal relations. Division of social duties. Duties of justice and charity.
Duties of justice.—Respect for life, liberty, honor, reputation, property, opinions and beliefs of others. Sacred character of promises and contracts.
Civil duties.—The State, foundation of public authority. National sovereignty, its limitations (liberty of conscience; personal liberty; property). Universal suffrage. Legislative, executive and judicial powers.
Duties of citizens: Patriotism, obedience to the laws, taxation, military service, voting, education.

THIRD YEAR.

A. The first three months are devoted to a review.

B. PRACTICAL PEDAGOGY AND SCHOOL MANAGEMENT.

1. *Pedagogic organization.*—Classification of pupils; programs; time-tables; preparation of lessons. School *cahiers.* Compositions.
2. *Discipline.*—Class order. Rewards and punishments.
3. Authorities placed over the supervision and direction of public schools; relations of the teacher with each. Department regulation of public schools.
Laws, decrees and circulars, with special study of the organic law of October 30, 1886, and of the decree and instructions of January 18, 1887.
4. Leading pedagogues and their doctrines. Analysis of the most important works.

C. NOTIONS OF POLITICAL ECONOMY.

Production of wealth. Agents of production: material, work, economy, capital, property.
Circulation and distribution of wealth. Exchange, money, credit, wages and interest.
Consumption of wealth. Productive and unproductive consumption, the question of luxury; expenses of the State; taxation, the budget.

FRENCH LANGUAGE AND LITERATURE.

1. READING AND RECITATION.

Classic selections read aloud. Choice selections committed to memory. Supplementary reading assigned by master or chosen by student under his direction; written or oral analysis of selections.

2. GRAMMAR AND GRAMMATIC EXERCISES.

First year.—Rational study of French grammar.
Second year.—Thorough review with essential historic notions.
For each course, oral and written exercises in orthography, grammatic and logical analysis.

3. COMPOSITION.

First year.—One hour. *Second and third years.*—Two hours.

4. HISTORY OF LITERATURE.

One hour in third year.
First trimestre.—Origin. *Renaissance.*—First half of the 17th century.
Second trimestre.—Second half of the 17th century and the 18th to the Revolution.
Third trimestre.—The 19th century. Review.

HISTORY AND CIVICS.

FIRST YEAR.

HISTORY.

First trimestre.—Ancient history; Greece and the Orient.
Second trimestre.—Roman history.
Third trimestre.—Middle ages to 100 years' war.
N. B.—Historic notions of the Orient, Greece and Rome should relate particularly customs, beliefs, monuments, and the part taken in the development of civilization. Legends, anecdotes, biographies, descriptions and literary history are very important. Time should be reserved at each lesson for selections from great ancient writers, modern historians or travelers.

SECOND YEAR.

First trimestre.— From the 100 years' war to the Reformation.
Second trimestre.— From the Reformation to the Revolution of 1688.
Third trimestre.— From the Revolution of 1688 to the French Revolution.
N. B.— The most important events, inventions and discoveries.

THIRD YEAR.

First trimestre.— The Revolution and the Consulate.
Second trimestre.— The Empire and the Restauration.
Third trimestre.— From 1830 to 1875. Review.
N. B.— Instruction as in second year, except that one hour a week for one *trimestre* is devoted to civics. The instruction in civics is most thorough as regards national institutions, including the system of primary education.

GENERAL GEOGRAPHY.

FIRST YEAR.

Elementary notions of cosmography. General study of the earth. Explanation of geographic terms. The globe and maps.

General study of the continents and oceans. Great orographic and hydrographic systems. Atmospheric and marine currents. Human races. Equatorial, tropical and polar regions.

Political geography. Particular study of the principal countries of Asia, Africa, America and Oceanica.

Principal geographic explorations.

SECOND YEAR.

GEOGRAPHY OF EUROPE.

General study of Europe.—Physical description. Particular study of each country (France not included): Physical, administrative, agricultural, industrial and commercial geography. Governments; religions.

THIRD YEAR.

GEOGRAPHY OF FRANCE.

Physical geography. Boundaries. Orography and hydrography. Historic and administrative geography: Ancient and modern divisions. Government (central, departmental and communal). Agricultural, industrial and commercial geography.

Geography of Algeria and of the French colonies. Physical and administrative geography. Agricultural and industrial products. Importation and exportation.

ARITHMETIC.

FIRST YEAR.

Operations with whole numbers. Divisibility by 2, 5, 4, 25, 3, 9, 11. Greatest common divisor; least common multiple. Common and decimal fractions. Metric system. Ratio and proportion. Simple interest. Discount. Exchange. Partnership. Alligation. Short methods in oral and written work.

SECOND YEAR.

A. Completion of arithmetic.
B. Algebra through equations of the first degree.

THIRD YEAR.

A. Algebra.— Solution of equations of the second degree with one unknown quantity. Applications to arithmetic and geometry. Arithmetic and geometric progressions. Logarithms. Compound interest and annuities.
B. Bookkeeping.— Single and double entry. Dispositions of the commercial code relative to commercial responsibility.

GEOMETRY.

FIRST YEAR.

Two books of Legendre.—Proportional lines. Similitude.

SECOND YEAR.

Length of the circumference. Measure of areas. Parallel lines and planes. Trihedral angles. Measure of volumes. Cylinder, cone, sphere.

THIRD YEAR.

Summary notions of trigonometry.
Construction of geometric plans. Scale. Conventional signs. Surveyor's compass, mariner's compass.
Practical work and problems in surveying. Levelling.
Dimensioned plans. Topographic plans and maps.
Topographic promenades.

PHYSICS.

FIRST YEAR.

Weight and hydrostatics.—Direction of weight. Center of gravity. Weights. Balances. Specific gravity. Liquids in equilibrium. Liquid pressure. Communicating vessels. Hydraulic press. Principle of Archimedes. Areometers. Gases. Atmospheric pressure. Barometers. Mariotte's law. Manometers. Pneumatic machines. Pumps; siphon. Balloons.

Acoustics.—Propagation of sound. Measure of the velocity of sound in the air, in liquids and in solids. Reflexion of sound. Qualities of sound.

SECOND YEAR.

Heat.—Dilation. Thermometers. Coefficients of dilation. Common applications. Conductivity. Applications. Motion in liquids and gases. Marine currents. Winds. Chimneys. Ventilation. Changes in the state of bodies. Fusion, solidification, dissolution, crystallization. Vaporization in air and in a vacuum. Vapors. Tension. Hygrometry. Clouds and fogs, rain, snow, frost. Evaporation. Ebullition. Distillation. Experimental notions of calorimetry. Freezing mixtures. Cold produced by evaporation. Manufacture of ice. Principal methods of heating in domestic economy and in industry. Idea of steam engines. Installation and observation of thermometers. Maxima and minima temperatures. Atmospheric pressure. Diurnal and annual variations. Winds. Weather indications. Cyclones. Blizzards.

THIRD YEAR.

Electricity and magnetism.—Production of electricity. Electric machines. Leyden jars. Atmospheric electricity. Batteries. Electric current. Electric light. Magnets. Compasses. Galvanometer. Magnetic Induction. Electro-magnet. General idea of the electric telegraph. Induction. Telephone.

Optics.—Propagation of light. Umbra and penumbra. Properties of plane and spheric mirrors established experimentally. Refraction. Prisms. Reflection; *mirage*. Properties of lenses, established experimentally. Magnifying glass. Microscope. Telescope. Decomposition and recomposition of light. Spectra. Rain-bow. Radiant heat.

Physical mechanics.—Motion. Inertia. Forces. Laws of the fall of bodies. Atwood's machine. Mass. Measure of force. Simple machines. Lever. Pulley. Motive power. Resistance. Notions of the equivalence of mechanic work and heat.

CHEMISTRY.
FIRST YEAR.
Analysis and synthesis of water. Hydrogen. Oxygen. Analysis of air. Nitrogen. General notions of chemical combustion. Disengaged heat. Change of properties. Principles of nomenclature and of chemical notation. Acids. Bases. Oxides of nitrogen. Nitric acid. Ammonia. Laws of chemical combinations. Chlorine. Hydrochloric acid. Iodine. Sulphur. Sulphuric acid. Sulphurous acid. Hydrosulphuric acid. Phosphorus. Phosphoric acid. Phosphoretted hydrogen. Carbon. Carbonic oxides. Carbonic acid. Silicic acid.

SECOND YEAR.
Metals. Alloys. Salts. Notions of equivalents. Potassium and sodium. Potash. Soda. Sea salt. Artificial salt. Calcium and magnesium. Lime; carbonate, sulphate, phosphate. Aluminum. Alumina. Alum. Silicates, clays, pottery and glass, lime, mortars, cements. Iron, zinc. Oxides, sulphates, carbonates. Notions of metallurgy. Tin, copper, lead. Oxides, sulphates and carbonates. Mercury, silver, gold, platinum

THIRD YEAR.
Summary notions of elementary analysis and synthesis of organic substances. The classification of these substances:
Hydro-carbon. Alcohol. Ether. Glycerine. Glucose. Dextrine. Phenol. Acids. Alkalies. Albumen. Gelatine. Preservation of woods, hides and foods.

THE NATURAL SCIENCES AND HYGIENE.
FIRST YEAR.
a. The description of the structure of the organs of plants.
b. Functions of nutrition, fecundation and germination.
c. Division of plants into dicotyledonous, monocotyledonous, and acotyledonous. Special study of useful and poisonous plants.

SECOND YEAR.
ZOOLOGY.
a. Anatomy and physiology of man.
b. Classification of animals.

THIRD YEAR.
GEOLOGY.
General study of the principal geologic phenomena of the present epoch.
Utilization thereof in the explanation of geologic phenomena of former periods.
Rocks. Geologic forces. Historic geology.
N. B.—Though the instruction in botany is placed in the first year of the course, nevertheless the students of the second and third years as well as those of the first are to make frequent botanic excursions under the direction of the professor.

HYGIENE.
Water. Air. Foods. Contagious diseases. Excrements. Sanitary conditions of the household. Diseases contracted at school. Vaccination and revaccination. Hygiene in infancy. Diseases of animals.

MODERN LANGUAGES.
FIRST YEAR.

Professors are not to lose sight of the fact that instruction in modern languages is for conversational purposes.
Simultaneous exercises in reading, writing and orthography.
Lists of words, exercises in conversation on these words.
Memory exercises, short and easy poems.
Pronunciation is to receive careful attention.
Instruction in grammar is to be practical in character.
Simple exercises in reading. Explanation of selections read.
Grammatic themes.

SECOND YEAR.

Continuation of the same method and exercises.
Lists of words and conversation on these words.
Memory exercises. Short and easy selections in prose and poetry.
Reading of choice selections. Conversation on selections read.
Continuation of grammar. Give a practical character to this instruction.
Short compositions on simple subjects. Letters.
Read in German Hebel's Schatzkästlein, Grimm's popular stories; In English, one of the readers and Miss Edgeworth's stories.

THIRD YEAR.

Continuation of the same method and exercises.
Oral and written exercises on lists of words.
Memory exercises: Selections chosen from the principal authors.
Exercises in reading.
Exercises in calculation in the foreign tongue.
Conversations on geography, travels and subjects connected with every-day life.
Review of the grammar.
Composition: Letters, descriptions, simple narratives.
Reading: Schiller's Geschichte des Abfalls der vereinigten Niederlande and Geschichte des dreissigjährigen Kriegs; Franklin's Autobiography; Miss Corner's History of England.
Songs in the foreign tongue throughout the course.
Extracts from foreign pedagogic journals.

AGRICULTURE.
SECOND YEAR.

a. Vegetable growth.—Study of the soil and means of modifying its chemical composition and physical properties; grains, leguminous plants, fodder, industrial plants.
b. Alimentation.—Domestic animals.
c. Rural economy and notions of agricultural accounts.

THIRD YEAR.
HORTICULTURE.

a. General notions.
b. Culture of trees.—Grafting.
c. The kitchen-garden.

The professor should dwell particularly on the horticultural conditions of the locality.

DRAWING.
FIRST YEAR.
IMITATIVE DRAWING.
The course of study closely resembles that of upper primary schools.

GEOMETRIC DRAWING.
The course of study is similar to that in upper primary schools.

SECOND YEAR.
Review with development as in upper primary schools.

THIRD YEAR.
Review of the work of the second year with development as in the upper primary schools.

N. B.—The development of the course of the upper primary schools is in the line of fitting the normal school students to teach the several divisions of the subject.

VOCAL AND INSTRUMENTAL MUSIC.
FIRST YEAR.
Elementary principles of music. Pronunciation and diction. Use of the voice. Respiration. Classification of voices. Exercises in major and minor scales.
Easy exercises in dictation. Execution of simple selections.
Elementary exercises on the organ or piano.

SECOND YEAR.
Review with development.
Oral and written exercises in major and minor scales in the keys of *sol* and *fa*.
Execution of selections in several parts.
Continuation of the exercises on the organ or piano.

THIRD YEAR.
Execution of choral music.
Elementary study of accompaniments and of harmony in connection with school songs.
Continuation of the exercises on organ or piano.
Notions of the history of music and of the principal master-pieces in music.

GYMNASTICS AND MILITARY EXERCISES.
FIRST YEAR.
GYMNASTICS.
Games. Promenades. Evolutions. Lessons in French boxing, stick and cane exercises. Fencing.
Exercises with gymnastic apparatus. Swimming.

MILITARY EXERCISES.
Formation of the section. Alignments. Marches. Countermarches.

SECOND YEAR.
GYMNASTICS.
Review with development. Rowing.

MILITARY EXERCISES.
Formation in open order. Deploying. Rallying. Mustering. Target practice.

THIRD YEAR.
GYMNASTICS.
Review and completion of the preceding exercises and methodic preparation for instruction in gymnastics in lower primary schools.

MILITARY EXERCISES.
School of the soldier with arms. Target practice. Study of the gun, model 1874.

NORMAL SCHOOLS FOR FEMALES.
1. PSYCHOLOGY. PEDAGOGY. MORALS.
The program is the same as in the normal schools for males, except that the professor is to dwell particularly on the duties of the wife, the mother and the housekeeper.

2. FRENCH LANGUAGE.
The same program as in normal schools for males.

3. HISTORY.
The same program as in normal schools for males.

HISTORY AND CIVICS.
THIRD YEAR.
The same program as in normal schools for males with less development.

GEOGRAPHY.
The same program as in normal schools for males.

MATHEMATICS.
The course includes arithmetic, plane geometry, and bookkeeping, with less development than in normal schools for males.

PHYSICS AND CHEMISTRY.
The course is simpler than that in normal schools for males. Instruction is essentially experimental and practical.

NATURAL SCIENCES.
In botany, zoology and hygiene the courses are the same as those in normal schools for males.
The course in geology is simplified.

DOMESTIC ECONOMY.
THIRD YEAR.
The household.— Care of dwelling and furniture. Care of clothing and linen. Washing and ironing. Alimentation. Nutritive qualities of different foods. Household accounts.

N. B.— The students are to be exercised as much as possible in the preparation of food and in other household duties.

Modern Languages.

The same program as that in normal schools for males.

Needlework.
First Year.

The making and care of garments.
The making of various articles of clothing for men, women and children by hand, or with the sewing machine.

Second Year.

Manner of taking measurements.
The study of patterns.
The drawing of patterns and the cutting of articles of clothing therefrom.

Third Year.

Review and completion of the first and second years.

Drawing.

The course is very similar to that in normal schools for males except that the applications to a certain extent are those adapted to work which is generally done by women.

Singing and Instrumental Music.

The same program as that in the normal schools for males.

Gymnastics.

The course of study is similar to that of normal schools for males with the omission of certain exercises.

CONCLUSION.

Several authorities have asserted that the French admit the superiority of Prussian schools, because French parents have sent their children in many cases to Prussian secondary schools. This argument had force as far as secondary schools were concerned, but it should have been restricted to these schools.

If France continues to make as much progress in her secondary schools as she has made during the past few years, the comparison with those of her rival will be as favorable as in the case of elementary schools. At present she is endeavoring to avoid the objections which have been urged by Germans against their own system of secondary instruction, and seems to be working along better and more practical lines, though it must not be overlooked that this work in France is yet in its infancy.

Schools, like prophets, are often not without honor save in their own country. We have many examples of the truth of this statement. Parents in New York often send their children away to be educated, when they would receive better instruction in the public schools at home. In the same way German parents send their children to France and French children are sent to Germany, though in these cases the acquisition of a modern language is often the principal reason.

We must also bear in mind the fact that the reputation of Prussian schools has been established for more than half a century, while the French system of public instruction dates almost entirely from the Franco-Prussian war, and in a large measure from 1882. The schools of Prussia have been perfected gradually from 1813, the date of the completion of the reorganization of the system of education.

With this fact in mind we do not expect to find such a high degree of perfection in the French as in the Prussian schools, and are indeed surprised that comparisons, based on results attained in so short a time are so favorable.

There is no system of public instruction which is not weakened by poor schools. I have heard lessons in technical grammar in Kindergärten in Paris, and I have visited second and third rate schools in Germany. When pupils have expressed surprise that as an American I was neither red nor black, and asked what language was generally spoken in the United States, I have not drawn general conclusions as to faulty methods of instruction because my other visits had convinced me that Prussian and French elementary schools have attained uniform degrees of excellence while our model elementary schools are exceptions to the rule.

It has been stated by prominent authorities that the French or Prussian child of 12 is about two years in advance of the American of the same age. It is most unjust to make such comparisons unless they are accompanied by explanations. It is not because the French or Prussian pupils have greater natural capacity than the American, but simply because from their sixth or seventh year of age they have been forced to attend school regularly for at least 40 weeks annually, and have been protected in school as far as possible from the imposition of bad work.

In France and in Prussia the laws fix a minimum of instruction for elementary schools, and surround the schools with all safeguards. The result is that the general standard of the work accomplished approaches that maintained in our best elementary schools.

In New York the laws do not prescribe the work for elementary schools. Each school is practically a law unto itself as to what shall be pursued and how. Furthermore, the legal school year is about ten weeks shorter than in Prussia and France, and attendance is irregular. The result is that our model elementary schools are exceptions to the rule.

www.ingramcontent.com/pod-product-compliance
Lightning Source LLC
Chambersburg PA
CBHW030320170426
43202CB00009B/1089